AQA GCSE (9–1)
English Literature
and Language

An Inspector Calls

Student Guide

Julia Burchell and Lindsay Skinner

Collins

William Collins' dream of knowledge for all began with the publication of his first book in 1819. A self-educated mill worker, he not only enriched millions of lives, but also founded a flourishing publishing house. Today, staying true to this spirit, Collins books are packed with inspiration, innovation and practical expertise. They place you at the centre of a world of possibility and give you exactly what you need to explore it.

Collins. Freedom to teach.

Published by Collins
An imprint of HarperCollins*Publishers*
The News Building
1 London Bridge Street
London
SE1 9GF

Browse the complete Collins catalogue at
www.collins.co.uk

10 9 8 7 6 5 4 3 2 1

ISBN 978-0-00-824939-7

British Library Cataloguing-in-Publication Data

A catalogue record for this publication is available from the British Library.

Commissioning editor: Catherine Martin
In-house editor: Natasha Paul
Development editor: Sonya Newland
Copyeditor: Sue Chapple
Proofreader: Nikky Twyman
Text permissions researcher: Rachel Thorne
Photo researcher: Alison Prior
Cover designer: Ink Tank
Cover photos: (l) mauritius images GmbH/Alamy Stock Photo, (r) itanistock/Stockimo/Alamy Stock Photo
Internal designer: Ken Vail Graphic Design
Typesetter: Jouve India Private Limited
Production controller: Rachel Weaver
Printed and bound by: Grafica Veneta S.p.A.

MIX
Paper from
responsible sources
FSC www.fsc.org **FSC™ C007454**

Contents

Introduction

How to use this book

This Student Book is designed to support your classroom study of *An Inspector Calls*.

It offers an integrated approach to studying English Literature and English Language, to help you prepare for your AQA GCSE exams.

This book can be used as a 10-week programme, if desired, or dipped into throughout your course or for revision.

English Literature

The book includes two pre-reading chapters to introduce some of the play's key contexts and concerns.

Five chapters then guide you through the play in depth, with activities to build your understanding of the plot, themes, characters, language and structure of the play.

At the end of your reading, two whole-text revision chapters revisit key themes, characters and contexts to help you form your own interpretations of the whole play.

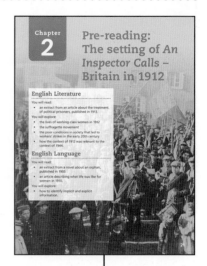

Each chapter opener page clearly shows you what you will read and explore for English Literature and for English Language.

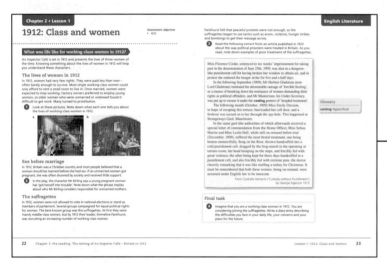

Literature lessons help you to engage with key scenes from the play, building your analysis skills.

Finally, Chapter 10 focuses on your Paper 2 English Literature exam. Three practice questions are provided, with guidance to help you plan and write effectively. Sample responses with commentaries show you the difference between a clear and well-explained and a convincing, analytical response.

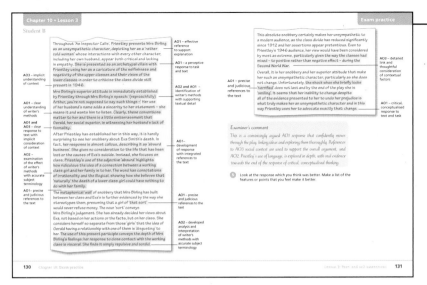

Practice questions and sample responses help you to prepare for assessment.

The closing page of each chapter offers a longer task on the text so far, to build your writing stamina for the final exam.

English Language

Each chapter also includes one or more lessons focused on building your English Language skills.

You will read fiction and non-fiction texts from the 19th, 20th and 21st centuries. These have been chosen to enhance your understanding of the themes and contexts of *An Inspector Calls*.

You will be given the opportunity to explore these texts and respond to them by answering questions in the style of the AQA Paper 1 and Paper 2 exams. Across the book, you will practise each of the AQA question types, including narrative, descriptive and discursive writing.

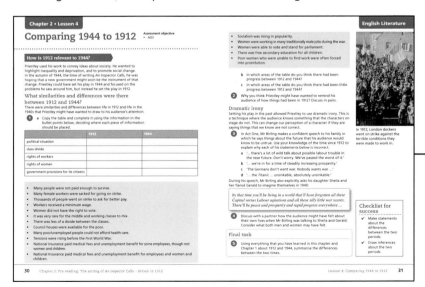

Language lessons will focus on one AQA question type. The text extracts have been chosen to deepen your understanding of the events, themes and contexts in this act of the play. Literature link boxes make the connection to the play clear.

Who's who? A guide to the main characters

Mr Arthur Birling

- Mr Birling is a prosperous manufacturer in his mid-50s, who believes in business and the importance of profit above anything else. He has married above himself and hopes to increase his social status further by being knighted in the next honours list, having been a Lord Mayor and a magistrate.

Mrs Sybil Birling

- Mrs Birling is from an upper-class background, 'superior' to that of her husband. As well as being a wife and mother to her two children, she is on the committee for the Brumley Women's Charity Organisation, which helps 'deserving' women in distress.

Sheila Birling

- Sheila is the daughter of Mr and Mrs Birling, in her early 20s and engaged to Gerald Croft.

Gerald Croft

- Gerald Croft is Sheila's fiancé and the son of Lord and Lady Croft, the owners of a local factory that competes with Mr Birling's. He is involved in his father's business and seems to share some of Mr Birling's beliefs.

Eric Birling

- Eric is the son of Mr and Mrs Birling, also in his early 20s. He is being trained in his father's business, without seeming to share his father's values. It becomes clear that Eric is rather wild and drinks a lot. Later we find out that he has stolen from his father.

Inspector Goole

- Inspector Goole presents himself as a police inspector, who has come to investigate the suicide of a girl called Eva Smith. He interrogates each of the characters in turn about their relationship to her.

- The Inspector appears halfway through Act One and drives the action of the play until he leaves partway through Act Three.

Eva Smith

- Eva Smith was a young working-class woman, whose parents had died. She had worked at and been sacked from Mr Birling's factory and then a clothes shop, before being forced to rely on the attention of men in the Palace Bar. She became Gerald's lover, then later Eric's, before falling pregnant with Eric's child. Having been refused help by Mrs Birling's charity, she took her own life and that of her unborn child.

- Eva Smith/Daisy Renton is only ever described by other characters.

Edna

- Edna is the Birlings' maid, who is seen in Act One clearing the table and announcing the Inspector's arrival.

Act summaries

Summary of Act One

The Birlings, a rich family, are having a dinner to celebrate their daughter Sheila's engagement to Gerald Croft. Mr Birling, the father, makes a speech in which he explains how pleased he is that Sheila is marrying Gerald Croft, whose father owns a rival business. He looks forward to the two families perhaps working together in the future.

As the women leave the men to port and cigars, the maid Edna enters to announce the arrival of a police inspector. The Inspector introduces himself and explains he is here to investigate the death of a young woman who killed herself that afternoon by drinking disinfectant.

This woman, Eva Smith, was employed at Mr Birling's factory. The Inspector's questions reveal that Mr Birling had sacked her 18 months before for organising a strike. Birling refuses to see anything wrong with his actions.

Sheila comes in to find what has happened to the men. The Inspector explains why he is here. Sheila is horrified to learn of Eva's death and her father's part in it. The Inspector tells them what happened to Eva after she left the factory: she was happy to get a new job as a shop assistant, but lost the job when a customer complained about her. Sheila is upset. The Inspector shows her a photo of the girl and Sheila runs out of the room. Her father follows, to find his wife. When Sheila returns, she explains she was the customer who had Eva sacked, because she had been jealous of the shop assistant's good looks and thought Eva had been laughing at her.

Sheila is full of regret.

The Inspector tells them that Eva then changed her name to Daisy Renton. Gerald seems surprised and startled. Eric takes the Inspector to find his parents, leaving Sheila and Gerald alone. Sheila asks Gerald how he knew Eva (Daisy) and whether she was the reason they hardly saw each other the previous summer. Gerald apologises and begs Sheila not to tell the Inspector.

The door opens and the Inspector returns.

Summary of Act Two

The Inspector begins to question Gerald. Gerald wants Sheila to leave the room, but she refuses. Mrs Birling enters and tries to get rid of the Inspector. Sheila intervenes to stop her mother and, as they argue, it is revealed that Eric is drunk and has been drinking too much for the last two years. Mr Birling comes back in and Gerald's interrogation begins.

Gerald explains that he met Daisy Renton in the Palace Bar, a place where men go to meet 'women of the town'. Daisy had stood out because she was young and pretty and Gerald had stepped in to rescue her from another man. They had a drink together and Daisy told him her story. Feeling sorry for her, Gerald offered to let her stay in a friend's flat while he was away. Gradually they became lovers. When the summer was over, the friend returned and the affair came to an end. The Inspector reveals that Eva used the money she had saved to spend two months in a seaside town remembering her time with Gerald.

Gerald is upset and moves towards the door. Sheila stops him and gives him back her engagement ring. They agree to talk later.

Now, the Inspector turns to Mrs Birling and shows her the photograph. Mrs Birling says she doesn't recognise the girl. Once again Sheila tries to persuade her mother to cooperate with the Inspector. Mr Birling leaves the room to find Eric.

The Inspector asks Mrs Birling about her work for the Brumley Women's Charity Organisation, and a meeting two weeks before.

Mr Birling returns; Eric is missing. The Inspector says he will need to be interviewed too.

Under questioning, Mrs Birling tells the Inspector a young woman calling herself 'Mrs Birling' had applied to the charity for help. At first she pretended her husband had deserted her, but eventually she admitted she was unmarried. Mrs Birling disapproved and refused to help.

The Inspector tells them the woman had been expecting a baby. It wasn't Gerald's baby.

Mrs Birling told the young woman that the father should take care of her. The Inspector reprimands her for turning the woman away, and Sheila agrees. Even Mr Birling worries that her actions might create a scandal if there is an inquest.

Mrs Birling reveals that the father was young and wild and drank too much. Eva told her he had stolen money and offered it to her, but she had refused to accept it. Mrs Birling once again blames the father of the child and says he should be made to publicly confess his guilt. Sheila tries to stop her talking, realising who the father might be …

Mrs Birling and her husband, beginning to realise too, look scared.

The front door opens and Eric steps into the room.

Summary of Act Three

Eric admits his guilt and tells the story of how he met Eva in the Palace Bar. He was drunk. At his insistence, they had gone home together to her lodgings and had sex. They met again a few times, again as Eric wanted to have sex with her. Soon afterwards, she told him she was pregnant. Eric had offered to marry her, had offered her money – money he had stolen from his father's office.

Sheila tells Eric what their mother did; how she persuaded her charity not to help Eva when she had applied for help. Eric is angry and upset.

The Inspector sums up what each of them did to lead Eva Smith to suicide. He tells them to reflect on the millions of other Eva Smiths and John Smiths whose lives are connected to theirs.

He leaves.

Once he has gone, the family argue, blaming each other. Mr Birling is worried the death will cause a public scandal.

Then they begin to question who the Inspector really was. Was he a police inspector?

The doorbell rings. It's Gerald. He also suspects that Inspector Goole was not a policeman. Mr Birling rings the Chief Constable and confirms this.

Even though the family agree that the whole evening must have been some sort of hoax, Eric and Sheila argue that this doesn't change what they each did wrong or the fact that a young woman is dead. Mr Birling now questions this fact and rings the hospital to find out if it is true. No one has died from drinking disinfectant that day.

Just as the older couple begin to relax, the telephone rings. It is the police. A girl has just died, on her way to the hospital, after drinking disinfectant. A police inspector is on his way to ask some questions …

Chapter 1

Pre-reading: The context of *An Inspector Calls* – post-war Britain

English Literature

You will read:

- extracts from J. B. Priestley's political writings.

You will explore:

- J. B. Priestley's life and concerns
- the society in which *An Inspector Calls* is set
- the lives and roles of women before and during the Second World War
- poverty and politics during and after the Second World War.

English Language

You will explore:

- how to plan descriptive writing
- the use of discourse markers to structure writing.

J. B. Priestley's life and concerns

Assessment objective
• AO3

Why did J. B. Priestley write *An Inspector Calls*?

Who was J. B. Priestley?

Knowing something about J. B. Priestley will help you to understand his motivation for writing *An Inspector Calls*. It will also help you explore the ideas, themes and characters in the play.

Here are some facts about Priestley's life before he wrote *An Inspector Calls*.

* J. B. Priestley was born in 1894. As the son of a schoolmaster he had a comfortable, but not luxurious, childhood.
* Priestley's father was the first schoolmaster to provide free school meals and baths.
* He was born in the Victorian era and died in 1984. During this period, Britain experienced massive social changes, particularly concerning the movement between classes and the role of women in society.
* He began writing while in his first job as a clerk. He wrote a regular column in a Labour Party magazine called the *Bradford Pioneer*.
* He fought in the First World War and was severely injured, spending months in hospital before going back into war as an officer.
* After the war he attended Cambridge University.
* Priestley read books about, and attended lectures about, time and the ability to see/alter the future.
* In 1934, he travelled around Britain to write a **travelogue** about the life of the working classes during the **Great Depression**.
* During the Second World War, he delivered a weekly radio broadcast, inspiring patriotism but also calling for social change, particularly more support for the working classes.
* He was part of a group that set up the Common Wealth Party in 1942. This was a movement to stop the private ownership of land and to promote democracy.
* He stood for election as an independent MP in the 1945 election.

Key terms

travelogue: a book about the experiences of a traveller as they visit different places

Great Depression: a severe economic depression marked by years of high unemployment

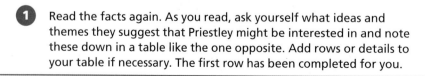

1. Read the facts again. As you read, ask yourself what ideas and themes they suggest that Priestley might be interested in and note these down in a table like the one opposite. Add rows or details to your table if necessary. The first row has been completed for you.

Priestley's interests and concerns	Evidence from his life
Education	His father was a schoolmaster.

Priestley's politics

Now look at some extracts from J. B. Priestley's political writings.

A

I have tried to make myself – and other people – aware of the harsh economic realities of our time. Again and again I have taken my typewriter to the factories, the mines, the steel mills. I denounced or jeered at those colleagues who would not look. I wrote some of the first detailed accounts of the depressed areas. Having been brought up on the edge of it, I knew what life was like 'back o' the mill'.

From *Delight*, an illustrated collection of essays about finding happiness, 1949

B

I am always hearing middle-class women in London saying that they could do with a change. They should try being a miner's wife in East Durham.

From *English Journey*, a travelogue, 1934

C

It was not the danger … but the conditions in which the lower ranks of the **infantry** were condemned to exist month after month … drained away health, energy, spirit … I went into that war free of any class feeling. No doubt I came out of it with a chip on my shoulder…

From *Margin Released*, Priestley's memoir, 1962

Glossary
....
infantry: foot soldiers

D

We're not fighting to restore the past; it was the past that brought us to this heavy hour.

From *Postscripts*, Priestley's BBC radio show, 1940

E

But the point is, now, at this moment, or any moment, we're only cross-sections of our real selves. What we really are is the whole stretch of ourselves, all our time, and when we come to the end of this life, all those selves, all our time, will be us – the real you, the real me. And then perhaps we'll find ourselves in another time, which is only another kind of dream.

From *Time and the Conways*, 1937

F

Britain, which in the years immediately before this war was rapidly losing such democratic virtues as it possessed, is now being bombed and burned into democracy.

From *Out of the People*, his views on British society and its reconstruction after the war, 1941

G

For the last twenty years we have been governed for the benefit of the **City**, and it does not follow that what sustains the City is the best for the sustenance of the nation.

From *Time and the Conways*, 1937

H

We cannot go forward and build up this new world order, and this is our war aim, unless we begin to think differently. One must stop thinking in terms of property and power and begin thinking in terms of community and creation. Take the change from property to community. Property is the old-fashioned way of thinking of a country as a thing, and a collection of things in that thing, all owned by certain people and constituting property; instead of thinking of a country as the home of a living society with the community itself as the first test.

From *Postscripts*, 1940

Glossary

City: London and London's financial sector

I

I grew up among socialists. I watched the smoke thicken and the millionaires who made it ride away. I saw broken old women creep back to the mills, and young men wither because there was no work for them to do and nobody wanted them. I saw the saddest waste of all, the waste of human life.

From *Delight*, 1949

J

I still feel today and must go on feeling until I die, the open wound, never to be healed, of my generation's fate, the best sorted out and slaughtered … The tradition of an **officer class**, defying both imagination and common sense, killed most of my friends as surely as if those **cavalry generals** had come out of the **chateau** with **polo mallets** and beaten their brains out.

From *Margin Released*, 1962

Glossary

officer class: the class of people who became officers – usually the middle class

cavalry generals: generals in the army who fought on horseback

chateau: a large French castle or country house

polo mallets: large wooden mallets used in the game polo, which is played on horseback

2 For each extract above, note down what you think Priestley is saying. Ask yourself:

- Is he describing something he dislikes?
- Is he explaining a belief that he has?
- Is he pointing out a problem in his society?

Final task

Priestley wrote *An Inspector Calls* in just one week in the autumn of 1944. In the play, he expresses many of his social and political views. In July 1945, Britain had a general election and Priestley stood as an independent MP.

3 In groups, discuss the ways in which you think Priestley wanted the new government to help change society in 1945. Consider the themes and ideas you have collected from the other tasks in this lesson.

1945: War and women

Assessment objective
• AO3

How did the lives and roles of women change during the Second World War?

It is important to understand the relationship between the text and the **context** in which in which it was written. This will help you better understand Priestley's reasons for writing the play.

Priestley grew up in Bradford, where he witnessed much poverty. Women were forced to work in factories in poor conditions for low pay. He described how he saw 'broken old women creep back to the mills'. The experiences of women like this feature in *An Inspector Calls*.

The role of women before the Second World War

An Inspector Calls was written in 1944, during the Second World War.

1 Read the following facts about British society before the Second World War. For each fact, write a sentence that explains what you think the impact would have been on women's lives.

   a The 1902 Education Act led to the opening of over 1000 secondary schools – 349 of which were for girls.

   b In 1908, the vacuum cleaner was invented, although it was a luxury item.

   c The 1919 Sex Disqualification (Removal) Act ruled that women could have professional careers, including as accountants, vets and lawyers.

   d The 1919 Sex Disqualification (Removal) Act ruled that women could sit on juries and become **magistrates**.

   e In the 1928 version of the **Book of Common Prayer**, women agreed to 'obey' their husbands in their wedding vows.

   f Many jobs had a 'marriage bar', which meant that women had to stop working once they were married.

The role of women during the Second World War

During the Second World War, women were employed to do many of the jobs that men had previously done.

2 Look at the photographs and artefacts on the next page. Write down what each one shows and what it tells you about the lives and roles of women during the Second World War.

Key terms

context: the social, cultural and historical influences on a writer, or the background to a text

magistrate: a person who acts as a judge in court, dealing with less serious crimes

Book of Common Prayer: the official service and prayer book used by members of the Church of England

a  b  c  d

The pay gap between women and men

During and after the Second World War, women were paid 53 per cent less than men to do the same jobs.

3 Discuss with a partner why you think women were paid less and what this says about the perceived value of women during this period.

4 In *An Inspector Calls*, we hear how the character Eva fights for better pay for herself and the women she works with. Is she right to do so? Discuss this with your partner. Give reasons for your opinion.

5 Imagine that you are a working woman during the Second World War. Write a list of what you hope will happen after the war. You might like to consider the following:

- war and peace
- your role at work and at home
- the attitudes of men
- your pay
- your family.

Final task

6 Copy and complete the table below to show how the war affected the lives of women. An example has been given to start you off.

The role of women before the Second World War	The role of women during the Second World War	How this may have affected women
Women were meant to 'obey' their husbands.	*Men were at war, so women had to look after themselves.*	*They might have felt that they were able to make their own decisions and did not need to 'obey' men any more.*

1945: Poverty and politics

Assessment objective
• AO3

How did the Second World War change the political landscape in Britain?

In *An Inspector Calls*, Priestley shows how capitalist values cause misery for the poor. He promotes socialist values as an alternative.

Capitalism and socialism

Capitalism is where private individuals own trade and industry. They are trying to make a profit. Socialism is where trade and industry are owned by the state and the profits are used to benefit the whole of society.

Britain is a capitalist country. However, some of its systems can be described as socialist, including the National Health Service (NHS), which is owned by the state and is intended to benefit everyone.

1 Read the following views from *An Inspector Calls* and note down whether they are more socialist or more capitalist.

   a 'A man has to make his own way.'

   b 'Everybody has to look after everybody else.'

   c 'A man has to mind his own business and look after himself and his own.'

   d 'We are members of one body.'

   e 'It's my duty to keep labour costs down.'

   f 'It's better to ask for the earth than to take it.'

Poverty and politics during the Second World War

In 1942, the Beveridge Report was published, outlining what needed to be done after the war to help Britain get back on its feet. The report stated that there were five 'giants', or enemies, that Britain needed to defeat:

• want
• disease
• ignorance
• squalor
• idleness.

2 Look up each of these words in a dictionary. Using your own words, write down what they mean.

The welfare state

The Beveridge Report proposed the creation of a **welfare state** – a government-funded system to help tackle the five 'giants'.

In 1945, the newly elected Labour government began to implement five types of support that were set out in the Beveridge Report in order to create a welfare state:

- **Social security:** this included introducing child benefit, sick pay and six months of unemployment pay.
- **National Health Service:** doctors' surgeries, hospitals, dentists and opticians were made free for all people to use.
- **Education:** secondary schools were made free and children were not allowed to leave before the age of 15 (1944).
- **Housing:** 1.25 million council houses were built.
- **Employment:** the government nationalised the railways, road haulage, and coal and steel industries, creating many jobs.

3 Discuss with a partner each type of support included in the welfare state. Decide which 'giant' from the Beveridge Report it tackled and how it would have helped people.

Class after the Second World War

Before the Second World War, there was a deep class divide in Britain. Many well-off middle-class people owned businesses that exploited members of the working class, paying them low wages in order to increase profits.

After the war, many people's views on class had changed and people of different classes began to mix more. This was due to several factors:

- Middle- and working-class men had fought together in the First and Second World Wars.
- In the Second World War, many children had been **evacuated** to families from a different class to their own.
- Middle- and working-class women had worked together during the Second World War.
- Many men of both classes returned home disabled.
- During and after the war, the government implemented **rationing** for all citizens.
- Everyone had experienced five years of war.

4 Write down how you think each factor in the list above would have changed people's attitudes to class.

Final task

5 Write a description of the changes that working-class people experienced after the Second World War. Include an explanation of why you think they occurred.

Key term

welfare state: a government-funded system designed to protect the health and wellbeing of its citizens, particularly people in financial or social need

Key term

evacuated: moved out of cities, where there was a danger of bombing, to live with families in the countryside

rationing: a fixed number of key things (often food) allowed to each person

Paper 1 Question 5: Description

Assessment objective
• AO5

How can I effectively plan a description inspired by a picture?

For Paper 1 Question 5 of your English Language exam, you will be asked to write either a description or a narrative. You will often be given a picture as a stimulus to help you with the task.

Thinking about atmosphere

First, look at the picture and simply think about what atmosphere and feelings it evokes. For example, in the picture here the atmosphere is bleak and pitiful – the image feels depressing.

1 Look at the picture on the right. Note down the atmosphere and feelings it evokes.

Planning your description

You will need to plan and write about six paragraphs. It may be helpful if your first and last paragraphs focus on the image as a whole. This technique is called 'bookending'. For the middle four paragraphs, select elements of the picture to focus on. You may find that drawing circles around these elements on the paper helps you choose the details to explore in each paragraph.

For the picture above, your plan might look like this:

Paragraph 1: The overall settlement: bleak, pitiful, depressing.

Paragraph 2: The pathway: broken, dry, scattered with litter.

Paragraph 3: The trees: leafless, dead, dry, dark.

Paragraph 4: The houses: dark, empty, cold.

Paragraph 5: The church: distant, smoggy, hopeful.

Paragraph 6: The overall settlement: bleak, pitiful, depressing – but it is home.

2 For the image in Task 1, decide which details you would focus on, then write a six-point plan, based on the example at the bottom of page 18.

Using discourse markers

Discourse markers are words or phrases that help organise writing and guide the reader through the text. In descriptions, writers often use **prepositional phrases** of time and place as discourse markers. These help link ideas and paragraphs, and make the writing fluent.

3 Read the description below. With a partner, identify the prepositional phrases and decide whether they are phrases of place or time.

> In the late afternoon, the chill begins to grow, seeping through the thin walls of the makeshift houses. Inside, it is dark and damp; people rub their hands together but to no avail. The cold seems inescapable. Huddling under blankets, families try to keep warm, quietly shivering.

To use discourse markers in your own writing, look at the picture and decide where the things you are going to focus on are positioned in relation to each other. Then add the prepositional phrases to your plan. For example:

> **Paragraph 1:** In the late afternoon, the overall settlement: bleak, pitiful, depressing.
>
> **Paragraph 2:** Under the grey sky, the pathway: broken, dry, scattered with litter.
>
> **Paragraph 3:** Above, the trees: leafless, dead, dry, dark.
>
> **Paragraph 4:** Inside the houses: dark, empty, cold.
>
> **Paragraph 5:** On the horizon, the church, distant, smoggy, hopeful.
>
> **Paragraph 6:** At nightfall, the overall settlement: bleak, pitiful, depressing – but it is home.

4 Using your plan you wrote earlier, add prepositional phrases to it to link your ideas.

Final task

5 Write a plan for the following question:

Write a description suggested by the image on page 12.

Key term

prepositional phrase: a phrase that explains where or when something is (e.g. the monster waited *under the bed*).

Checklist for success

✔ Plan for six paragraphs.

✔ Think about the atmosphere of the picture and the feelings it evokes.

✔ 'Bookend' your plan to structure your description.

✔ Use discourse markers to link your paragraphs.

End of chapter task

Priestley's life experiences, and the society in which he was born and lived, would have significantly influenced his outlook and therefore the themes and ideas he decided to write about.

 Write a summary of the key factors that influenced Priestley's writing. Draw together ideas from across this chapter. You could write a paragraph on each of the following:

- poverty
- the First World War
- the class divide
- the Second World War
- the role of women in society
- the Beveridge Report and the welfare state.

Check your progress

- I can clearly explain the context in which Priestley was writing.
- I can clearly explain how the context influenced Priestley's writing.

- I can thoughtfully consider the context in which Priestley was writing.
- I can thoughtfully explain how the context influenced Priestley's writing.

Chapter 2

Pre-reading: The setting of *An Inspector Calls* – Britain in 1912

English Literature

You will read:

- an extract from an article about the treatment of political prisoners, published in 1913.

You will explore:

- the lives of working-class women in 1912
- the suffragette movement
- the poor conditions in society that led to workers' strikes in the early 20th century
- how the context of 1912 was relevant to the context of 1944.

English Language

You will read:

- an extract from a novel about an orphan, published in 1905
- an article describing what life was like for women in 1910.

You will explore:

- how to identify implicit and explicit information.

1912: Class and women

Assessment objective
• AO3

What was life like for working-class women in 1912?

An Inspector Calls is set in 1912 and presents the lives of three women of the time. Knowing something about the lives of women in 1912 will help you understand these characters.

The lives of women in 1912

In 1912, women had very few rights. They were paid less than men – often barely enough to survive. Most single working-class women could only afford to rent a small room to live in. Once married, women were expected to stop working. Factory owners preferred to employ young women, so older women who were unmarried or widowed found it difficult to get work. Many turned to prostitution.

 Look at these pictures. Note down what each one tells you about the lives of working-class women in 1912.

a    b

Sex before marriage

In 1912, Britain was a Christian country and most people believed that a woman should be married before she had sex. If an unmarried woman got pregnant, she was often shunned by society and received little support.

 In the play, the character Mr Birling says a young pregnant woman has 'got herself into trouble'. Note down what the phrase implies about who Mr Birling considers responsible for unmarried mothers.

The suffragettes

In 1912, women were not allowed to vote in national elections or stand as members of parliament. Several groups campaigned for equal political rights for women. The best-known group was the suffragettes. At first they were mainly middle-class women, but by 1912 their leader, Emmeline Pankhurst, was recruiting an increasing number of working-class women.

Pankhurst felt that peaceful protests were not enough, so the suffragettes began to use tactics such as arson, violence, hunger strikes and bombings to get their message across.

 3 Read the following extract from an article published in 1913 about the way political prisoners were treated in Britain. As you read, note down examples of poor treatment of the suffragettes.

Miss Florence Cooke, sentenced to six weeks' imprisonment for taking part in the demonstration of June 25th, 1909, was shut in a dungeon-like punishment cell for having broken her window to obtain air, and in protest she endured the hunger strike for five and a half days.

In the following September (1909), Mr Herbert Gladstone (now Lord Gladstone) instituted the abominable outrage of 'forcible feeding', as a means of breaking down the resistance of women demanding their rights as political offenders, and Mr Masterman, his Under-Secretary, was put up to excuse it under the **canting** pretext of 'hospital treatment'.

The following month (October, 1909) Miss Emily Davison, in hope of escaping this torture, barricaded her cell door, and a firehose was turned on to her through the spy-hole. This happened in Strangeways Gaol, Manchester.

In the same gaol (the authorities of which afterwards received a special letter of commendation from the Home Office), Miss Selina Martin and Miss Leslie Hall, while still on remand before trial (December, 1909), suffered the most brutal treatment, one being beaten unmercifully, flung on the floor, thrown handcuffed into a cold punishment cell, dragged by the frog-march to the operating or torture-room, her head bumping on the steps, and forcibly fed with great violence; the other being kept for three days handcuffed in a punishment cell, and also forcibly fed with extreme pain, the doctor cheerily remarking that it was like stuffing a turkey for Christmas. It must be remembered that both these women, being on remand, were assumed under English law to be innocent.

From *Custodia Honesta* ('Custody without Punishment')
by George Sigerson 1913

Glossary

canting: hypocritical

Final task

 4 Imagine that you are a working-class woman in 1912. You are considering joining the suffragettes. Write a diary entry describing the difficulties you face in your daily life, your concerns and your plans for the future.

1912: Poverty and politics

Assessment objective
- AO3

What led to the workers' strike in the early 20th century?

Through *An Inspector Calls*, Priestley explores workers' rights and factory owners' responses to strikes. To fully understand the play, therefore, it is important to know something about the politics of the time in which it is set – 1912.

Poverty and politics in 1912

1 Look at the images and facts below. For each one, write a description of what it shows or says. Then add a comment to explain what each suggests about society in 1912.

a

b

c | The National Insurance Act 1911 was one of the first steps towards the creation of the welfare state. It set up a national system of insurance, protecting working people against illness and unemployment.

d | The coal strike of 1912 was the first national strike by coal miners in Britain. Its main goal was securing a minimum wage. After 37 days, the government intervened and ended the strike by passing a minimum wage law.

e | When the luxury passenger ship Titanic sank in 1912, it was carrying only enough lifeboats for 52 per cent of its passengers. The higher the class of person, the more likely they were to be allocated a lifeboat: 62 per cent of first-class passengers found places in the lifeboats, compared with 41 per cent of second-class passengers and 25 per cent of third-class passengers.

f | In 1911, the UK **census** showed that the richest 1 per cent of the population owned 70 per cent of Britain's wealth.

The Great Unrest

Between 1911 and 1913, there were several serious industrial conflicts in Britain, with thousands of workers going on **strike**. This period became known as the 'Great Unrest'.

 The **trade union** movement continued to grow and many strikes occurred, attempting to improve workers' rights. Research the strikes between 1900 and 1914 and create a timeline of key events or facts. Use the three facts below to help you.

- In May 1912, the **dockers'** strike came to an end, with no gains made for the workers.
- In 1912, nearly 1 million miners went on strike, demanding a minimum wage.
- In 1914, almost all strikes stopped, due to the outbreak of the Second World War.

 An Inspector Calls is set in 1912. In the play, the character Mr Birling says that there will be no more strikes. Use the data below to write an explanation of why he is wrong.

Key terms

census: an official survey of a population and details of their lives

strike: when people in a certain industry stop working in protest at the conditions of their employment

trade union: a group of workers that come together to protect and further the rights of workers

docker: a person who works on the docks

Year	1900	1901	1902	1903	1904	1905	1906	1907	1908	1909	1910	1911	1912
Labour disputes annual estimates	3088	4130	3438	2320	1464	2368	3019	2148	10785	2687	9867	10155	40890

Year	1913	1914	1915	1916	1917	1918	1919	1920	1921	1922	1923	1924	1925	1926
Labour disputes annual estimates	9804	9878	2953	2446	5647	5875	34969	26568	85872	19850	10672	8424	7952	162233

Final task

In *An Inspector Calls*, we learn how Eva Smith, a factory worker, led a group of female workers to strike, asking for more money. As the ringleader, she was sacked by the factory owner, Mr Birling.

 Using the information from this lesson about poverty and politics in the early 20th century, write a short evaluation of how Mr Birling's actions were typical of the time.

Paper 1 Question 1 and Paper 2 Question 1: Identifying information

Assessment objective
• AO1

Paper 1 Question 1: Finding explicit information

Paper 1 Question 1 of your English Language exam will ask you to read a short section of a fiction extract and to list four things about a topic from it. You are only expected to find *explicit* information – information that is clearly stated in the text.

To complete this question, you will need to follow some simple steps:

- **Step 1:** Read the question and highlight the topic you need to focus on.
- **Step 2:** Identify the line references in the question to ensure that you only select information from the specified section.
- **Step 3:** Reread the section and underline information that relates to the topic in the question.
- **Step 4:** From the points that you have underlined, select the four most relevant ones to write down.
- **Step 5:** Write each one down in a clear, short sentence. You can choose whether to include quotations.

1 Read the following extract from a longer text, then answer the question by choosing the four most relevant points and writing a sentence about each one. Use the steps above, but leave out Step 2.

In this extract, Sara has just become an orphan. She goes to the room she now has to live in with her doll, Emily.

List four things from this part of the text about the room.

> The room had a slanting roof and was whitewashed. The whitewash was dingy and had fallen off in places. There was a rusty grate, an old iron bedstead, and a hard bed covered with a faded coverlet. Some pieces of furniture too much worn to be used downstairs had been sent up. Under the skylight in the roof, which showed nothing but an oblong piece of dull gray sky, there stood an old battered red footstool. Sara went to it and sat down. She seldom cried. She did not cry now. She laid Emily across her knees and put her face down

upon her and her arms around her, and sat there, her little black head resting on the black draperies, not saying one word, not making one sound.

From *A Little Princess* by Frances Hodgson Burnett, 1905

Paper 2 Question 1: Finding implicit information

For Paper 2 Question 1, you will have to identify both explicit and implicit information. Implicit information will require you to make **inferences**.

The question will list eight facts based on the opening of a text. You need to decide which four of the facts are true. To complete this question, you will need to follow some simple steps:

- **Step 1:** Identify the line references in the question to ensure that you only select information from the specified section.
- **Step 2:** Read each statement in turn and decide whether you think it is true or false. Some of the statements will be explicit information and straightforward to identify. If you are sure about a statement, mark down whether it is true or false.
- **Step 3:** Consider the statements you are unsure about. Look at key words in the statements and try to find them in the specified section. Look out for **synonyms** or **antonyms** of the key word. For example, if the statement was about people being equal, you should also look for 'superior', 'inferior' or 'second class'.
- **Step 4:** If you are unsure about some statements, think about whether what they say matches with the overall message of the extract. This may help you decide whether they are true or false.
- **Step 5:** If you cannot decide whether some statements are true or false, guess rather than leave the question blank.
- **Step 6:** Before you move on to the next question, double check that you have only marked four statements as true.

Key terms

inference: working out what a writer has suggested by reading between the lines

synonym: a word that is close in meaning to another word (e.g. wet/damp)

antonym: a word that is opposite in meaning to another word (e.g. wet/dry)

2 Read the first part of the source on the next page, from lines 1 to 22, and answer the question using the steps above.

Choose four statements below which are true.

1 Women were treated as men's equals in 1910.

2 Middle-class women had the most difficult lives.

3 Some lower-class girls attended private school.

4 Working-class girls did get to study geography or history.

5 Working as a maid paid more than working in industry.

6 Many working-class girls needed to get married to survive.

7   Men did not want women to join the workforce, as they thought it would bring down wages.

8   Many of the wives who were stuck in poverty lived in the city.

Everywoman in 1910: No vote, poor pay, little help – Why the world had to change

All women in 1910, irrespective of social class ... , were seen as second-class citizens – a fact underlined by the denial to them of the parliamentary vote. And all women were encouraged from childhood to strive to the ideal of serving others, to consider the interests of their menfolk first rather than their own. Since most women were expected to become full-time
5   wives and mothers, rather than earn their own living, options in life were limited. This was especially so for ordinary, working-class girls and women who had fewer choices than their middle-class sisters and lived lives of toil and drudgery.

Working-class girls who attended state elementary schools were taught a limited curriculum. Lessons focused on the 3 Rs (reading, writing and arithmetic), a little geography
10 and history, and a large chunk of domestic subjects, such as needle-work, house management, cookery, laundry work and childcare.

Although the age of compulsory school attendance had been raised to 14 in 1899, many working-class girls left a year earlier, on possession of a labour certificate to enter dead-end, poorly-paid jobs, especially in domestic service. The lowest paid was the maid-of-all-work or
15 general servant, earning £12 to £18 a year, plus board and lodging. Other single working-class women might earn 13 shillings a week (65p) in the non-textile industries, but even that was not enough for a fully independent existence.

Marriage became a practical necessity for working-class women, few of whom wanted to be left on the shelf. Once married, working-class husbands were usually against their wives
20 going out to work, believing that a family wage was the way to earn respectability – and keep their wages high. But most wives lived in a cycle of poverty, especially in urban areas where working-class families lived in damp, dark, overcrowded **tenements** infested with bugs. Such conditions took their toll on the health of all the family, but women were hardest hit. They scrimped and scraped, often depriving themselves of food to buy a 'relish' for a husband's tea or
25 bacon for his breakfast.

[…]

It was the deplorable state of working-class women's lives that prompted Emmeline Pankhurst, in 1903, to found the Women's Social and Political Union (WSPU), a women-only organisation that was to campaign for the vote for women. She believed the lack of the vote was
30 the key factor underpinning the inferior status of women in **Edwardian** Britain and they 'would remain a servant class until they lifted themselves out of it'. The campaign her suffragettes fought was never a single issue campaign but a broad-based reform movement that sought to bring equality for women in the family, education, employment and the law.

From 'Everywoman in 1910', *The Mirror*, 2010

20th-century tenement buildings in Glasgow

Literature link
....

This article describes what life would have been like for working-class women in 1912, when *An Inspector Calls* is set. It shows why Eva had to try so hard to do well in her job and to get a pay rise.

Final task

 Using what you have learned about Question 1 on both Paper 1 and Paper 2, create a revision card that outlines what the questions will ask you to do and the approach you should take.

Comparing 1944 to 1912

Assessment objective
• AO3

How is 1912 relevant to 1944?

Priestley used his work to convey ideas about society. He wanted to highlight inequality and deprivation, and to promote social change. In the autumn of 1944, the time of writing *An Inspector Calls*, he was hoping that a new government might soon be the instrument of that change. Priestley could have set his play in 1944 and focused on the problems he saw around him, but instead he set the play in 1912.

What similarities and differences were there between 1912 and 1944?

There were similarities and differences between life in 1912 and life in the 1940s that Priestley might have wanted to draw to his audience's attention.

 a Copy the table and complete it using the information in the bullet points below, deciding where each piece of information should be placed.

	1912	1944
political situation		
class divide		
rights of workers		
rights of women		
government provisions for its citizens		

- Many people were not paid enough to survive.
- Many female workers were sacked for going on strike.
- Thousands of people went on strike to ask for better pay.
- Workers received a minimum wage.
- Women did not have the right to vote.
- It was very rare for the middle and working classes to mix.
- There was less of a divide between the classes.
- Council houses were available for the poor.
- Many poor/unemployed people could not afford health care.
- Tensions were rising before the First World War.
- National Insurance paid medical fees and unemployment benefit for some employees, though not women and children.
- National Insurance paid medical fees and unemployment benefit for employees and women and children.

- Socialism was rising in popularity.
- Women were working in many traditionally male jobs during the war.
- Women were able to vote and stand for parliament.
- There was free secondary education for all children.
- Poor women who were unable to find work were often forced into prostitution.

b In which areas of the table do you think there had been progress between 1912 and 1944?

c In which areas of the table do you think there had been little progress between 1912 and 1944?

2 Why you think Priestley might have wanted to remind his audience of how things had been in 1912? Discuss in pairs.

Dramatic irony

Setting his play in the past allowed Priestley to use dramatic irony. This is a technique where the audience knows something that the characters on stage do not. This can change our perception of a character if they are saying things that we know are not correct.

3 In Act One, Mr Birling makes a confident speech to his family in which he says things about the future that his audience would know to be untrue. Use your knowledge of the time since 1912 to explain why each of his statements below is incorrect.

a '... there's a lot of wild talk about possible labour trouble in the near future. Don't worry. We've passed the worst of it.'

b '... we're in for a time of steadily increasing prosperity.'

c 'The Germans don't want war. Nobody wants war ...'

d '... the *Titanic* ... unsinkable, absolutely unsinkable.'

During his speech, Mr Birling also explicitly asks his daughter Sheila and her fiancé Gerald to imagine themselves in 1940:

> *by that time you'll be living in a world that'll have forgotten all these Capital versus Labour agitations and all these silly little war scares. There'll be peace and prosperity and rapid progress everywhere ...*

4 Discuss with a partner how the audience might have felt about their own lives when Mr Birling was talking to Sheila and Gerald. Consider what both men and women may have felt.

Final task

5 Using everything that you have learned in this chapter and Chapter 1 about 1912 and 1944, summarise the differences between the two times.

In 1912, London dockers went on strike against the terrible conditions they were made to work in.

Checklist for success

✔ Make statements about the differences between the two periods.

✔ Draw inferences about the two periods.

End of chapter task

An Inspector Calls includes a range of characters from different classes. Each character's role is informed by the context of 1912.

1 Look at the following details about each character and rank them from the most powerful (1) to the least powerful (6) according to their social status. For the character you put at number 6, write a short paragraph explaining why you consider their role to be the one with the least power.

Sheila: an upper-middle-class woman in her early 20s.

Eric: an upper-middle-class man in his early 20s.

Arthur Birling: an upper-middle-class man and business owner in his mid-50s.

Eva Smith: a young working-class woman.

Sybil Birling: an upper-class woman in her 50s.

Gerald Croft: an upper-class man about 30 years old.

Check your progress

- I can clearly explain how gender, poverty and politics affected people's lives in 1912.
- I can clearly explain the relationship between 1912 and 1944.

- I can thoughtfully consider how gender, poverty and politics affected people's lives in 1912.
- I can thoughtfully consider the relationship between 1912 and 1944.

Chapter 3

Act One:
Meet the Birlings

English Literature

You will read:

- from the beginning of Act One until Mrs Birling, Sheila and Eric exit.

You will explore:

- the setting of the play
- the character of Mr Birling
- the theme of the younger generation.

English Language

You will read:

- an extract from a novel about the *Titanic* disaster.

You will explore:

- how to analyse the effect of language.

The setting of An Inspector Calls

Assessment objectives
- AO1, AO2, AO3

Text references
You will have read from:
- the beginning of the play to the end of the first set of stage directions.

> How does understanding setting help my study of *An Inspector Calls*?

The location of *An Inspector Calls*

The play is set in Brumley, a fictional industrial city in the North Midlands. In the 1900s, this area of England was dominated by iron, steel and coal production. Many workers lived close to the factories in terraces of small houses. Local shops and pubs would have catered to the needs of these workers.

1
  a Discuss with a partner how this location suggests a particular mood or atmosphere for the play.

  b Note down any particular types of events or action that might feature in a play set in this location. (Consider the events and issues you learned about in Chapter 2.)

'The dining-room of a fairly large suburban house'

The Birling house is described in Priestley's stage directions as being a 'fairly large suburban house belonging to a prosperous manufacturer'.

 Think about the language used by Priestley to describe the house and its owner. Copy and complete the following table. The first row has been done for you.

Language choice	What it means ...	What you think of	What you feel	What you imagine
'suburban'	It is on the outskirts of the city.	A affluent area with spacious, expensive houses and large gardens.	It must be a nice place to live. The family there are fortunate.	The family living there must be quite well off.
'fairly large'				
'prosperous'				

In the stage directions, Priestley states that the Birling house is in 'Brumley, an industrial town in the North Midlands'.

 Think about the setting of the Birling house in the industrial Midlands. In pairs, discuss what the contrasts between the town and the house might be. Consider:

- what conditions might be like in the industrial town
- what kind of people may live in the town and what their lives would be like
- what conditions might be like in the 'large suburban house'
- what kind of people may live in the house and what their lives would be like
- what you feel about the contrast between the two places and the people.

Priestley gives a precise description of the dining room in which the play is set. This suggests that it is not just a backdrop but a key element that will influence other parts of the play.

Look closely at the stage directions below, taken from the start of Act One. They contain some clues about the social class and status of the people who live there.

> EDNA, *the parlourmaid, is just clearing the table*

The aristocracy would often have more than 10 servants to run a large house. The middle classes would have at least one female servant to do heavy work, and often a cook as well.

> ... *replacing them with decanter of* **port**, *cigar box and cigarettes*

Glossary

port: a fortified red wine (with spirits added) that is made in Portugal

In Edwardian times, it was traditional for the women to leave the dining room after a meal, while the men remained there to smoke and drink port or **claret** with their coffee. In 1912, some hostesses were beginning to ignore this 'rule'.

> *All five are in evening dress of the period, the men in tails and white ties, not dinner-jackets.*

White tie was a traditional form of dress, at first worn by the aristocracy and then copied by the men who gained wealth through industry. A dinner jacket was a more comfortable and less formal alternative.

4 Select one or more key words from each of the quotations above. Use these to create a spider diagram, with the word(s) in the middle and their **connotations** around the outside. It can help to think of connotations as the effect of word choices. The first one has been done for you.

Key terms

claret: a red wine from Bordeaux in France
connotation: an idea or emotional association that a word or phrase has, in addition to its literal or primary meaning

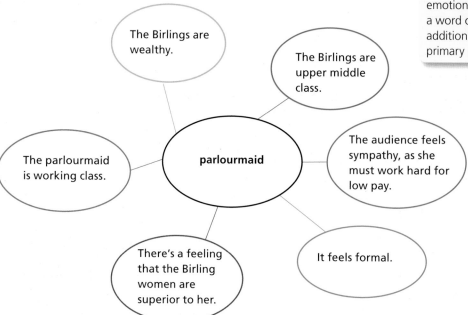

The Birlings are wealthy.

The Birlings are upper middle class.

The parlourmaid is working class.

parlourmaid

The audience feels sympathy, as she must work hard for low pay.

There's a feeling that the Birling women are superior to her.

It feels formal.

The *what*, the *how* and the *why*

It is useful to practise writing about the text in a way that meets Assessment objectives 1, 2 and 3:

- AO1: understand and respond to the text using textual detail/references.
- AO2: analyse the language, form and structure the writer uses, using subject terminology.

- AO3: show understanding of the relationships between texts and the contexts in which they were written.

Look at this short question:

How does Priestley establish the setting?

 Read the response below and discuss with a partner where it covers each Assessment objective.

> In the stage directions, Priestley uses **exposition** to establish the Birlings as an affluent, middle-class family. The setting, their 'dining room', demonstrates that they have specifically decided to spend their wealth on objects that reflect their class: 'good solid furniture'. The adjective 'solid' suggests that the furniture is made of an expensive hardwood, conveying their wealth. This wealth is further emphasised by the 'decanter of port'. Port is an expensive drink, associated with large meals. It is drunk with dessert so the port implies that they have eaten a meal with dessert, which many families in 1912 would not have been able to afford. Moreover, the fact that they have a 'decanter' indicates that this is a drink that is often consumed in their house.

Key term

exposition: a detailed explanation of a situation or event

Your response to an exam question about character or theme will need to cover the *what*, the *how* and the *why*:

- **What (AO1):** Explain *what* ideas you have about the character or the theme in the question. This includes ideas that are both explicit and implicit.

- **How (AO2):** Explain *how* the writer has presented these ideas – for example, the words they have chosen, the language devices they have used or how they have structured the text.

- **Why (AO3):** Explain what the writer's purpose was – *why* they decided to present a character or theme in a particular way. To do this well, you need to understand the context of the text and its writer and consider it thoughtfully in order to make a judgement about the writer's motives.

How comments should include the following features:

- **subject terminology**
- the effect or connotations of individual words or language devices
- comments on the effect of structure.

Key term

subject terminology: the specific name of a word class or a device used by the writer (e.g. adjective, noun, verb, past participle or simile, metaphor, personification)

 Reread the student response above and note down where it uses each of the features listed above.

Final task

7 Using your notes from this section and the paragraph above as an example, write your own paragraph in response to this question:

How does Priestley establish the setting?

Introducing Mr Birling

Assessment objectives
• AO1, AO2

Text references
You will have read from:
• the start of Act One up to where Mrs Birling, Sheila and Eric exit.

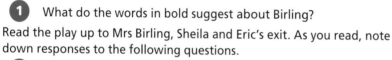

How does Priestley establish the character of Mr Birling?

Impressions of Birling

Our first impressions come from the stage directions. Priestley describes Birling explicitly, which suggests he wanted certain features to be unchangeable in performance.

> ARTHUR BIRLING *is a heavy-looking, rather* **portentous** *man in his middle fifties with fairly easy manners but rather* **provincial** *in his speech.*

 What do the words in bold suggest about Birling?

Read the play up to Mrs Birling, Sheila and Eric's exit. As you read, note down responses to the following questions.

   a   What does Birling value?

     b   What does he think of himself?

     c   How does he treat others?

What Birling represents

Writers use characters, settings and events as devices to develop the narrative or to explore themes or ideas.

 Look back at the information in Chapter 1 about Priestley's interests and concerns. Write a list of the themes and ideas you think that he is exploring through Birling. Consider the following:

- economics
- politics
- class
- sex/gender.

Priestley's undermining of Birling

In Chapter 2 (see page 31), you looked at how Priestley used dramatic irony, where Birling makes several assertions that Priestley's early audiences – and an audience today– would know to be wrong.

4   Choose one example of dramatic irony in Birling's speeches. Write a paragraph explaining what it makes the audience think about the character and his judgement.

Glossary

portentous: self-important or pompous; behaving and speaking more seriously than necessary to impress people

provincial: connected with parts of the country outside the capital city, narrow-minded and lacking the sophistication of city life

Birling sounds confident and assured, emphasising his certainty that he is right. This makes the audience question his judgement even further.

> *There's a lot of wild talk about possible labour trouble in the near future. Don't worry. We've passed the worst of it.*

adjective implies he thinks the talk is illogical and crazy

short, direct imperative implies that he is confident and in charge

use of an aphorism makes his opinion sound as though it is a fact.

5 Look at the examples of dramatic irony below. Select the words and devices that show Birling's assuredness.

> … you'll hear some people say that war's inevitable. And to that I say – fiddlesticks! The Germans don't want war. Nobody wants war …

> … the Titanic … unsinkable, absolutely unsinkable …

Key term

aphorism: a brief statement that contains a general truth about something

Final task

Priestley undermines Birling in other ways, too, presenting him as patronising and racist.

describing himself as 'hard-headed' makes him sound arrogant and unsympathetic to the workers, caring only about profit, not people

irony in saying 'must say something sometime' as this implies that he does not speak very often, when he is by far the most dominant speaker in the play; shows he lacks self-awareness

> *We hard-headed practical business men must say something sometime. And we don't guess – we've had experience – and we know.*

pronoun 'we' indicates that he is part of an elite group that no one else in the room is part of and understands

dashes imply he is pausing, enjoying having an audience and slowing his speech down to emphasise its importance

6 Look at the three quotations below. Copy each one and annotate it with comments about what it reveals about Birling's character, and how.

- There's a good deal of silly talk about these days – but – and I speak as a hard-headed business man, who has to take risks and knows what he's about
- Just let me finish, Eric. You've got a lot to learn yet.
- There'll be peace and prosperity and rapid progress everywhere – except of course in Russia, which will always be behindhand naturally.

The younger generation

Assessment objectives
- AO1, AO3

Text references
You will have read from:
- the start of Act One up to where Mrs Birling, Sheila and Eric exit.

How does the younger generation differ from the older generation?

Introducing Sheila and Eric

At the start of the play, it is clear that Mr Birling, representing the older generation, is the dominant character. He differs from his children, Sheila and Eric, who represent the younger generation.

1 Look at the descriptions of both younger characters in the stage directions. Other than their ages, note down any characteristics of the younger generation that Priestley includes.

Sheila and Eric interact with each other using playful language, which develops them as **sympathetic characters**. This contrasts with the way that the audience is manipulated against Birling from the start of the play.

2 Read from '*Eric suddenly guffaws*' to 'Actually, I was listening' and note down quotations that help form your first impressions of Eric and Sheila. Consider the following:

- their interaction with each other
- their interaction with their parents
- how they are presented as sympathetic characters.

Key terms

sympathetic character: a character the audience identifies and sympathises with

archetypal: typical

subservient: with characteristics of a servant, being below someone

Sheila as an Edwardian woman

Young women of the Edwardian era were supposed to be quiet and respectful. In some ways, Sheila is presented as the **archetypal** Edwardian woman, **subservient** to men. To a modern audience, Sheila may appear immature and controlled by the men around her.

3 Look at the following quotations and write an explanation of how they present Sheila as a traditional Edwardian woman.

> 'When do I drink?'
> 'Is it the one you wanted me to have?'
> 'I'm sorry, Daddy. Actually I was listening.'

By 1912, when the play is set, the women's suffrage movement (see pages 22–23) had begun to challenge the inferior position of women in society. There are signs that Sheila is not altogether a traditional Edwardian woman. At the dinner table, she speaks with confidence and playfulness to both Gerald and Eric.

 4 Discuss with a partner why you think Priestley shows Sheila as a young woman speaking confidently to the men around her. What might he be suggesting about the role of women at the time?

The way that the other characters react to Sheila is also revealing. Mrs Birling makes it clear that she does not approve of Sheila's behaviour:

> 'What an expression, Sheila! Really the things you girls pick up these days!'

She also clarifies what will be expected of Sheila when she is married:

> 'When you're married you'll realise that men with important work to do sometimes have to spend nearly all their time and energy on business. You'll have to get used to that, just as I had.'

5 Write a short explanation of how you think the 1946 audience would have reacted to Mrs Birling's words. Remember that, in 1945, many women had taken on responsible jobs while men were away at war.

Eric as an Edwardian man

As a young man in 1912, Eric was more likely than Sheila to speak confidently, because his place in society was more valued. However, he would have been expected to show resect to his elders, particularly his father.

6 Reread the opening part of the play and jot down quotations that show that Eric does not always show full respect to his parents. Consider where he:

- interrupts his father
- challenges his father's views
- asks questions.

7 With a partner, discuss why you think Priestley chose to show Eric challenging his father's views. What was Priestley saying about society and the views of the younger generation?

Final task

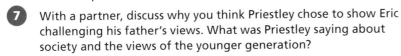

8 Write two paragraphs to answer the following question:

How and why does Priestley present the younger generation as different from the older generation?

Checklist for success

✔ Explain your first impressions of Sheila and Eric.

✔ Support your ideas with quotations.

✔ Comment on why you think Priestley presented them this way – what did he want the younger generation to represent?

Paper 1 Question 2: Use of language

Assessment objective
• AO2

How can I write about the effects of language?

Responding to questions about language

Paper 1 Question 2 will ask you how the writer has used language to achieve effects in a particular section of an extract, focusing on a particular topic.

Before you do anything else, identify the topic in the question. Be careful to focus on exactly what the question is asking you – it is easy to make your focus too wide. For example, if the question asks you to describe the effects of an explosion in the passage, do not just write about the explosion generally; you must focus on its *effects*.

 Read the questions below and note down the precise topic each question asks you to focus on.

   a How does the writer use language here to describe the effects of the weather?

   b How does the writer use language here to describe Lindsay's love?

   c How does the writer use language here to describe Julie's beauty?

   d How does the writer use language here to describe the atmosphere at the party?

The question will have three bullet points below it, which indicate elements you may wish to focus on. You could include the writer's choice of:

• words and phrases

• language features and techniques

• **sentence forms**.

You do not *have* to write about these, but they can be useful guidance if you are unsure what is meant by the term 'language'.

The easiest way to focus on language is to look at the devices and the individual words used by the writer. You will need to select words and phrases from the text that relate to the focus of the question, then comment on the effect of these words and phrases, using subject terminology.

To write about the effects of language, you need to focus on the connotations of words and devices. You should explain what the language choice makes you – the reader – think, feel and imagine.

> **Key term**
>
> **sentence forms:** sentences with different purposes, including imperative (instruction), interrogative (question) exclamatory (exclaiming) and declarative (stating)

Look at the following question:

How does the writer use language to describe the emotions of the girl?

 2 a Read the sentence below. Select a word or device that you think is effective. Note it down, labelling it with the correct subject terminology.

Her hopes shattered into unthinkably sharp pieces.

    b List all the effects it has, considering its connotations and what it makes the reader think, feel and imagine.

What will you get marks for?

You should aim to demonstrate the following three skills:

- using textual detail or a short quotation
- accurately using subject terminology
- exploring the effects of the language choice.

3 Read the student response below and note where you think each of the skills have been demonstrated. Which skill is *not* demonstrated?

> The writer describes the surface of the water as 'glittering'. This indicates that it is bright and shining, reflecting the light. It creates a peaceful and beautiful picture and I imagine a bright surface that seems as though it is sparkling as it moves.

The cumulative effect of language

To be awarded the highest marks for effect, you need to begin to explain the *cumulative* effect of language. This is how the effect of one word builds on the effect of another to develop a stronger overall image or atmosphere.

When writing about your selections, focus on one word and then link it to another word that helps to build on the effect. Here are some phrases to help you:

- The writer couples this language with . . .
- The cumulative effect of this is . . .
- The writer develops the image with . . .
- The writer builds the **semantic field** by using . . .

Key term

semantic field: a group of words used in a text that have similar connotations or create a similar effect

4 Read the extract below and note down any words that specifically imply that the man is still fighting.

In this extract, a man is on the deck of the Titanic as it is about to sink. It has already crashed into the iceberg and has taken on board large amounts of water. He, along with the rest of the passengers, is trying to escape alive.

The ship staggered and tipped, a great volume of water flowed over the submerged bows and tossed me like a cork to the roof. My fingers touched some kind of bolt near the ventilation grille, and I grabbed it tight. I filled my lungs with air and fixed my eyes on the blurred horizon, determined to hang on until I was sure I could float free rather than be swilled back and forth in a maelstrom. I wouldn't waste my strength in swimming, not yet, for I knew the ship was now my enemy and if I wasn't vigilant would drag me with her to the grave.

From *Every Man for Himself* by Beryl Bainbridge, 1996

Final task

 5 Read the extract below, from the same book, and answer the question. Allow 15 minutes to write your response.

In this extract, a man is in the water, clinging on to the Titanic *as it is about to sink. He is trying to escape the sinking ship and not drown.*

> I waited for the next slithering dip and when it came and the waves rushed in and swept me higher, I released my grip and let myself be carried away, over the tangle of ropes and wires and davits, clear of the rails and out into the darkness. I heard the angry roaring of the dying ship, the deafening cacophony as she stood on end and all her guts tore loose. I choked on soot and cringed beneath the sparks dancing like fire-flies as the forward funnel broke and smashed the sea in two. I was sucked under, as I knew I would be, down, down, and still I waited, waited until the pull slackened – then I struck out with all my strength.
>
> From *Every Man for Himself* by Beryl Bainbridge, 1996

How does the writer use language here to describe the sinking of the *Titanic*? You could include the writer's choice of:

* words and phrases
* language features and techniques
* sentence forms.

Literature link

These novel extracts describe the sinking of the *Titanic*, an event that occurred shortly after the time that *An Inspector Calls* is set in, and an event that Mr Birling swears was 'absolutely' impossible.

Checklist for success

✔ Only write about the focus of the question.
✔ Aim to write between three and four paragraphs.
✔ Use textual detail/quotations.
✔ Use accurate subject terminology.
✔ Explore the effect of individual words and devices.
✔ Comment on the cumulative effect of language.

End of chapter task

In contrast to Sheila and Eric, Mr Birling is established early on as a negative character. Consider the opening of Act One, and your responses to the questions in this chapter, then answer the following exam-style question:

 1 In the opening of Act One, how far does Priestley present Mr Birling as an unlikeable character? Write about:

- what Mr Birling says and does at the beginning of Act One
- how Priestley presents him by the way he writes.

Check your progress

- I can clearly explain my thoughts about character, supporting my points with quotations.
- I can clearly describe how Priestley's methods create character.
- I can show clear understanding of the upper middle class in 1912.

- I can write critically about character, supporting my points with judicious textual detail.
- I can analyse the ways in which Priestley's methods craft character.
- I can show thoughtful consideration of the upper middle class in 1912.

Chapter 4

Act One:
The catalyst and
the rising action

English Literature

You will read:

- Act One, from Mrs Birling, Sheila and Eric's exit until the end of the act.

You will explore: .

- the role of the Inspector as the catalyst
- how Priestley presents political ideas through Mr Birling.
- contrasts in the text and their effect on interpreting character.

English Language

You will read:

- an article about working conditions in the 19th century
- a webpage about working conditions in contemporary sweatshops in Bangladesh.

You will explore:

- how to identify and summarise information and make inferences.

Inspector Goole as the catalyst

Assessment objectives
- AO1, AO2

Text references
You will have read from:
- the start of Act One to where the Inspector says: 'her real name – was Eva Smith'.

Why is the arrival of Inspector Goole important?

Understanding narrative structure

Most narratives follow an arc, which marks how tension develops and is then resolved. There are six main parts to the narrative arc:

1 Copy the diagram and add the key events from the play so far to show where you think they belong on the arc.

Climax: The most intense and significant part of the narrative, often characterised by a dramatic event or realisation.

Rising action: A rising tension triggered by the catalyst (often the longest part of the narrative).

Catalyst: Something new changes the atmosphere of the story.

Falling action: Tension begins to fall away and events that have occurred are reflected upon.

Exposition: Setting and characters are introduced.

Resolution: The issues caused by the catalyst are resolved or concluded.

The arrival of the Inspector

The arrival of Inspector Goole alters the atmosphere of the play and leads to a change in plot direction – he is the catalyst. His arrival is signalled by a '*sharp*' ring of the doorbell. It interrupts Birling's speech, in which he declares: 'a man has to mind his own business and look after himself and his own'.

2 In pairs, discuss why Priestley included the sound effect of the doorbell during this speech. Consider the following:
- capitalism versus socialism
- the narrative arc
- the role the Inspector might have in the events to follow.

3 Why do you think Priestley wanted the doorbell to sound '*sharp*'? What connotations and effect does it have? What does it imply about the visitor?

Priestley describes the Inspector: '*he creates at once an impression of massiveness, solidity and purposefulness*'. The semantic field used to describe him is one of power.

4 Priestley uses three nouns in his description of Inspector Goole: *'massiveness'*, *'solidity'* and *'purposefulness'*. Note down the connotations of these nouns.

5 The paragraph below analyses Priestley's choice of the word *'massiveness'*. Read it, then write a similar paragraph for either *'solidity'* or *'purposefulness'*.

> Priestley's use of the noun 'massiveness' indicates that Inspector Goole is either a physically large character or that he appears large, perhaps due to his confidence. This impression of largeness depicts an intimidating character and suggests that his significant presence will change the atmosphere of the party.

Priestley indicates a change of **tone** when Inspector Goole arrives through the stage directions:

> *The lighting should be pink and intimate until the* INSPECTOR *arrives, and then it should be brighter and harder.*

Key term

tone: a writer's attitude or the nature of their 'voice' in a piece of writing

6 With a partner, discuss what this lighting effect suggests about the feelings of the Birlings before and after the arrival of Inspector Goole.

Before Inspector Goole arrives, the working class has only been referred to in abstract terms (as 'labour costs', for example). The Inspector changes this by bringing the reality of working-class life into the Birlings' home. Priestley contrasts the lives of the different classes with the Inspector's words: 'she'd swallowed a lot of strong disinfectant. Burnt her inside out, of course.'

7 What is the effect of the Birlings drinking champagne and port while Eva Smith is described as drinking 'strong disinfectant'?

Nomenclature

Nomenclature is the naming of things. Writers often choose names that say something about their characters. Inspector Goole's name is a play on the word 'ghoul'.

8 Using what you know about Inspector Goole so far, write a short explanation of why you think Priestley chose this name.

Checklist for success

✔ Make comments that show your understanding of the play.

✔ Comment on the effect of Priestley's language choices.

✔ Use quotations to support your points.

Final task

9 Answer the following question in three paragraphs.

What is the effect of the introduction of Inspector Goole to the Birlings' dining room? Consider the following:

- the timing of Inspector Goole's arrival
- Inspector Goole's description
- nomenclature.

Exploring capitalism through Mr Birling

Assessment objectives
- AO1, AO2, AO3

Text references
You will have read from:
- where Birling asks, 'Eva Smith?' up to where Sheila says, 'Yes, I expect it would.'

How does Priestley use Mr Birling to represent capitalism?

Birling's power and influence

As an upper-middle-class man in 1912, Birling would have had significant power and influence. Priestley shows him as a man who cares very much about his social position and who repeatedly tries to demonstrate his power over others.

 Copy and complete the table below to identify what tactics Birling uses to show his power, and to explain what this reveals about his character.

Quotation	What tactic(s) Mr Birling is using	What it suggests about Mr Birling
'Have a glass of port – or a little whisky?'	Being friendly and generous, as if it is a visiting friend.	He believes he is above the law and that his money will impress and persuade people to be on his side.
'I was an alderman for years – and Lord Mayor two years ago – and I'm still on the Bench.'		
'Just keep quiet, Eric, and don't get excited.'		
'Yes, well, we needn't go into all that.'		
'I don't like that tone.'		
'Look – just you keep out of this.'		

Mr Birling's capitalist views

Essentially, capitalists are in favour of the private ownership of companies to make profit. However, there are more extreme capitalist views, including the belief that profit is more important than any other consideration, including people.

In this part of the play, Birling describes his response when some of his factory workers, including Eva Smith, asked for a pay rise: 'I refused, of course.' He later explains his reasoning with the words: 'Well, it's my duty to keep labour costs down.'

2 Note down what Priestley's use of the **adverbial** 'of course' tell us about Mr Birling's views.

3 Write a short paragraph explaining how Priestley presents Mr Birling as having capitalist views in this section of the text. Consider:

- what capitalist views are
- what Birling considers to be important
- how what he says is capitalist.

Social responsibility

Social responsibility is the idea that every person has a responsibility to help and support everyone else, so that society as a whole can function well. In Birling's capitalist speech, he refers to socialist views as believing that 'everybody has to look after everybody else, as if we're all mixed up together like bees in a hive'.

4 Research how a beehive works, then discuss with a partner why you think Priestley used this **simile**.

Later, when Inspector Goole speaks to Birling about Eva, it is clear that the two men have very different attitudes towards social responsibility:

> BIRLING: Rubbish! If you don't come down sharply on some of these people, they'd soon be asking for the earth.
> [...]
> Inspector: They might. But after all it's better to ask for the earth than to take it.

5 How much does each man seem to care about the wellbeing of others? Which character is more socially responsible?

6 Note down what Birling's use of the words 'these people' to describe the workers suggests about his attitude towards them.

Key terms

adverbial: a word or phrase used to modify a verb or a clause

simile: a comparison between two things using the words 'as' or 'like'

Final task

Gerald supports Birling's capitalist views ('You couldn't have done anything else'), but Inspector Goole, Eric and Sheila all question them. In this way, Priestley begins to include socialist counter-arguments in the play.

7 Find these counter-arguments and note them down in a copy of the table below. Add a note of who says them.

Birling's capitalist views	Socialist views
'It's my duty to keep labour costs down.'	'Why shouldn't they try for higher wages? We try for the highest possible prices.' (Eric)
'We were paying the usual rates and if they didn't like those rates, they could go and work somewhere else.'	
'So she had to go.'	
'If you don't come down sharply on some of these people, they'd soon be asking for the earth.'	

Paper 2 Question 2: Summarising

Assessment objective
- AO1

What is the best way to summarise two texts?

Summarising similarities or differences

Paper 2 Question 2 will ask you to summarise *either* the similarities *or* the differences between two sources on a particular topic. You will need to write a short summary of both sources. You can write about each source separately but, equally, you can write about both sources together if you want to.

1 Read the question below and identify what you are being asked to summarise.

> You need to refer to Source A and Source B for this question.
>
> Use details from both sources to write a summary of the similarities in the working conditions described.

Summarising as an AO1 skill

Once you have identified the key parts of the question, you need to read the texts and apply your AO1 skills:

- making **statements** about the text
- supporting your statement with **textual detail** (quotations)
- making **inferences** from the detail you have selected.

2 Read Source A and select quotations that relate to the question.

Source A

In 1888, a socialist group called the Fabian Society met to discuss the matchbox company Bryant & May. At that meeting, they decided to not buy any matches from the company because of the poor pay and working conditions.

White slavery in London

The hour for commencing work is 6.30 in summer and 8 in winter; work concludes at 6 p.m. Half-an-hour is allowed for breakfast and an hour for dinner. This long day of work is performed by young girls, who have to stand the whole of the time. A typical case is that of a girl of 16, a **piece-worker**; she earns 4s. a week, and lives with a sister, employed by the same firm, who 'earns good money, as much as 8s. or 9s. per week'. Out of the earnings 2s. is paid for the rent of one room; the child lives on only bread-and-butter and tea, alike for breakfast and dinner, but related with dancing eyes that once a month she went to a meal where 'you get coffee, and bread and butter, and jam, and marmalade, and lots of it'; now and then she goes to the Paragon, someone 'stands treat, you know', and that appeared to be the solitary bit of colour in her life.

The splendid salary of 4s. is subject to deductions in the shape of fines; if the feet are dirty, or the ground under the bench is left untidy, a fine of 3d. is inflicted; for putting 'burnts' – matches that have caught fire during the work – on the bench 1s. has been forfeited, and one unhappy girl was once fined 2s. 6d for some unknown crime. If a girl leaves four or five matches on her bench when she goes for a fresh 'frame' she is fined 3d., and in some departments a fine of 3d. is inflicted for talking. If a girl is late she is shut out for 'half the day', that is for the morning six hours, and 5d. is deducted out of her day's 8d. One girl was fined 1s. for letting the web twist round a machine in the endeavour to save her fingers from being cut, and was sharply told to take care of the machine, 'never mind your fingers'. Another, who carried out the instructions and lost a finger thereby, was left unsupported while she was helpless. The wage covers the duty of submitting to an occasional blow from a foreman; one, who appears to be a gentleman of variable temper, 'clouts' them 'when he is mad'.

One department of the work consists in taking matches out of a frame and putting them into boxes; about three frames can be done in an hour, and ½d. is paid for each frame emptied; only one frame is given out at a time, and the girls have to run downstairs and upstairs each time to fetch the frame, thus much increasing their fatigue. One of the delights of the frame work is the accidental firing of the matches: when this happens the worker loses the work, and if the frame is injured she is fined or 'sacked'. 5s. a week had been earned at this by one girl I talked to.

From Issue No. 21 of *The Link: A Journal for the Servants of Man,* 1888

Once you have selected your quotations, annotate them with statements that relate them to the question. For example:

The women work very long hours.

'The hour for commencing work is 6.30 in summer and 8 in winter; work concludes at 6 p.m.'

Glossary

piece-worker: a worker who earns a fixed rate per piece they complete, regardless of how long it takes

s: shilling

d: pence

3 For each of your selected quotations, write a statement that relates it to the question.

In the exam, you would repeat this process for the second source, then identify the similarities and write about those.

Making inferences

To make inferences, you need to read between the lines, explaining what the quotation tells you that is not immediately obvious. You are not exploring the effects of individual word choices here – you need to explain the explicit and implicit meaning of the whole quotation. Two or three statements about each text will be enough. Marks are allocated on the quality of the statements and inferences, not how many you make.

4 Select the three quotations that you think are most interesting or from which you could make the best inferences. For each one, create a spider diagram to show the implicit information it contains.

> Key context
>
> After the article was published, Bryant & May tried to force their workers to sign a statement that said they were happy with their working conditions. When some women refused, they were sacked. In protest, 1400 women went on strike, gaining national attention. Eventually the company agreed to re-employ the women, improve conditions and remove the fines system.

Spider diagram:
- half their time working
- 'The hour for commencing work is 6.30 in summer and 8 in winter; work concludes at 6 p.m.'
- working through all of daylight
- no flexibility in hours

Writing your paragraph

Finally, you need to write your summary. To do this, turn your statements, quotations and inferences into sentences. For example:

> The workers have to work very long hours: 'The hour for commencing work is 6.30 in summer and 8 in winter; work concludes at 6 p.m.' This means that in the summer, nearly half of their day is spent working and, throughout the year, almost all of the daylight is taken up with work, meaning that the rest of their life would be spent in the dark. 'The hour for commencing work' sounds non-negotiable, implying that there is no flexibility in the working hours, indicating that the workers have little power and that their individual circumstances are not taken into consideration.

Final task

 5 Answer the following question using Source A and Source B. Spend five minutes reading Source B. Spend 15 minutes planning and answering the question.

You need to refer to **Source A** and **Source B** for this question.

Use details from **both** sources to write a summary of the **similarities** in the working conditions.

Source B

Sweatshops in Bangladesh

In Bangladesh, 3.5 million workers in 4,825 garment factories produce goods for export to the global market, principally Europe and North America. The Bangladeshi garment industry generates 80% of the country's total export revenue. However, the wealth generated by this sector has led to few improvements in the lives of garment workers, 85% of whom are women.

The majority of garment workers in Bangladesh earn little more than the minimum wage, set at 3,000 taka a month (approximately £25), far below what is considered a living wage, calculated at 5,000 taka a month (approximately £45), which would be the minimum required to provide a family with shelter, food and education.

As well as earning a pittance, Bangladeshi factory workers face appalling conditions. Many are forced to work 14–16 hours a day seven days a week, with some workers finishing at 3am only to start again the same morning at 7.30am.

On top of this, workers face unsafe, cramped and hazardous conditions which often lead to work injuries and factory fires. Since 1990, more than 400 workers have died and several thousand more have been wounded in 50 major factory fires.

Sexual harassment and discrimination is widespread and many women workers have reported that the right to maternity leave is not upheld by employers. Factory management also take steps to prevent the formation of trade unions, a right protected under the Freedom of Association and Collective Bargaining ILO Conventions, which Bangladesh ratified in 1972.

From 'Sweatshops in Bangladesh', War on Want

Checklist for success

✔ Keep your planning notes brief.
✔ Read the question carefully.
✔ Only write about similarities.
✔ Only write about the topic of the question.
✔ Make two to three statements of similarity for each text.
✔ Use quotations for each statement.
✔ Make inferences for each statement.

Understanding Sheila

Assessment objectives
- AO1, AO3

Text references
You will read:
- up to where Inspector Goole says, 'she changed her name to Daisy Renton'.

> ## How does Priestley contrast Shelia with other characters?

Sheila's response to the death of Eva Smith

After the Inspector has interrogated Mr Birling, Sheila enters the room. A stage direction shows the audience that she is immediately affected by Eva's story:

> '(*rather distressed*) Sorry! It's just that I can't help thinking about this girl'.

1 Note down how Sheila's reaction to hearing about Eva's death differs from Mr Birling's reaction.

As the Inspector tells Sheila about Eva, she continues to react strongly to the story, interrupting him with outbursts of emotion:

> 'I should think so. It's a rotten shame.'
> 'But these girls aren't cheap labour – they're people.'

2 Discuss with a partner what this reveals about the difference between the two characters. Look back to Lesson 4.2 to remind yourself of Mr Birling's attitude and ideas if you need to.

Sheila had an impact on Eva Smith's life without realising it.

3 Read the section from 'But what happened to her then?' to 'she changed her name to Daisy Renton'. Create a flow chart that shows the events that occurred after Eva Smith was sacked by Birling, to the point where she changed her name. Include key quotations in your chart.

Personal responsibility

Personal responsibility is the idea that people are responsible for their own actions and their consequences. It means that individuals can be held morally and legally accountable for what they have done. Some characters in *An Inspector Calls* take personal responsibility for their role in Eva Smith's death. Others do not.

Priestley uses Sheila's reactions to show clearly her attitude towards personal responsibility:

'(*miserably*) So I'm really responsible?'
'Yes, but it didn't seem to be anything very terrible at the time […]
And if I could help her now, I would—'
'It's the only time I've ever done anything like that, and I'll never, never do it again to anybody.'

4 What does this tell us about Sheila's character? How does this make you feel about her?

5 Copy and complete the table below to show the contrast between Sheila's views and those of her father.

Sheila	Mr Birling	How they differ
'So I'm really responsible?'	'Still, I can't accept any responsibility.'	
'I felt rotten about it at the time and now I feel a lot worse. Did it make much difference to her?'	'If you don't come down sharply on some of these people, they'd soon be asking for the earth.'	
'It's the only time I've ever done anything like that, and I'll never, never do it again to anybody.'	'I was quite justified.'	

6 Write a summary of the differences between the responsibility these two characters accept for the death of Eva Smith.

Sheila's life and Eva's life
As the Inspector tells Eva's story, the audience inevitably draws comparisons between her life and Sheila's life.

7 Consider the characters of Sheila and Eva. Note down the key differences between them. Consider the following: background, personality, how they are treated, the options available to them and their life events.

Checklist for success
✔ Explain what you think each character represents.
✔ Give quotations to support your points.
✔ Link your ideas to the social context of 1912.

Final task
8 Consider everything you have learned about Eva and Sheila so far. What do you think Priestley wanted each character to represent? Write 300 words explaining your thoughts. Consider:
- gender
- class
- age
- wealth.

End of chapter task

1 In the play so far, you have looked at how Birling and Sheila respond to the death of Eva Smith. Use the reading and notes you have made to answer the following question, based on the beginning of Act One to Inspector Goole's words: 'she changed her name to Daisy Renton'.

How does Priestley present views about the working class in *An Inspector Calls*? Write about:

- different ideas about the working class in *An Inspector Calls*
- how Priestley presents these ideas by the ways he writes.

Check your progress

- I can write clearly about ideas and tension in the play.
- I can clearly explain how Priestley's methods explore ideas and create tension.
- I can show clear understanding of the contextual factors that influenced Priestley's writing.

- I can write critically about ideas and tension in the play.
- I can analyse the ways in which Priestley's methods explore ideas and create tension.
- I can show thoughtful consideration of the contextual factors that influenced Priestley's writing.

Chapter 5

Act Two: Characters in their society

English Literature

You will read:

- Act Two.

You will explore:

- how Priestley uses the character of Gerald to comment on the society of the time
- symbolism in the character of Eva Smith.

English Language

You will read:

- an extract from a memoir from 1933 describing life for poor working-class people
- a letter sent to a magazine in 1889 arguing against female suffrage
- an article from a women's suffrage magazine in 1910 arguing in favour of women having the vote.

You will explore:

- how to analyse the effects of language in non-fiction texts
- how to compare writers' viewpoints and perspectives.

The role of Gerald

Assessment objectives
- AO1, AO2, AO3

Text references
You will have read from:
- the start of Act Two, to where the Inspector says: 'No. It wasn't necessary and I thought it better not to.'

How does Priestley use Gerald to make comments about society?

Gerald Croft, part of the aristocracy

At the beginning of the play, the audience's impressions are guided by Priestley, and certain aspects of Gerald's character are clearly fixed for any director of the play:

> 'Gerald Croft is an attractive chap about thirty, rather too manly to be a **dandy** but very much the **easy well-bred** young man-about-town.'

1 Note down the connotations and effects of Priestley's choice of 'easy', 'dandy' and 'well-bred' on the audience's interpretation of Gerald and his family.

2 Reread the beginning of the play. Jot down any evidence you can find that shows that Gerald is of a higher social status than Mr and Mrs Birling.

Gerald's views on the working class

Gerald's views on the working class seem to change depending on whether he is talking about the class generally or Daisy Renton (Eva Smith) specifically.

3 Look at the two groups of quotations below. How do Gerald's attitudes compare for each group?

Daisy Renton:

'She looked young and fresh and charming.'

'she felt I was interested and friendly'

'I was sorry for her'

The working class:

'They'd all be broke – if I know them.'

'I know we'd have done the same thing.'

4 **a** Look at Priestley's use of adjectives in the first set of quotations. What do they indicate about his thoughts and feelings?

b Look at Priestley's use of **pronouns** in the second set of quotations. What is the effect of the use of 'them' and 'we'.

5 When Gerald finishes telling the story of his relationship with Daisy Renton, he says he would like to leave because he is 'rather more – upset – by this business than I probably appear to be – and – well, I'd like to be alone for a while'.

What effect does each set of dashes have in this quotation?

Glossary

dandy: a middle-class person who behaved as if they were part of the aristocracy and spent their time on their appearance and pleasure

easy: easy-going – relaxed, calm and confident

well-bred: referring to a person's family history and their links to the upper classes as well as their good manners

Key term

pronoun: a word that replaces a noun or noun phrase (e.g. he, she, they, him, her)

Gerald's infidelity

At the beginning of the play, Gerald tells Sheila that he had been 'very busy at the works' the previous summer. At the end of Act One, however, we discover that this was a lie, when he admits to having an affair. After hearing that Gerald took Eva as his mistress, Sheila calls him 'the wonderful Fairy Prince'.

6 Do you think that Gerald is a prince or a villain? Copy and complete the table below to assess his behaviour.

Action	'Prince'	'Villain'
Goes to a bar which prostitutes use to meet men.		
Sees a pretty girl and looks at her.		
Realises the girl needs help getting away from Alderman Meggarty.		
Tells girl she needs to leave if she is to avoid being treated like a prostitute.		
Takes her for a drink at the County Hotel.		
Buys her a meal when he finds out that she is hungry.		
Arranges to meet her again.		
Offers her a place to go and money when he finds out that she is homeless and penniless.		
Visits her regularly and she becomes his mistress.		
Breaks off the relationship and gives her money as a parting gift.		

Final task

7 Write a 300-word essay response to the following question:

How does Priestley use the character of Gerald to explore the theme of class?

Write about:

- what Gerald says and does in the play
- how Priestley explores the theme of class through what Gerald says and does.

Checklist for success

✔ Consider the benefits and expectations of Gerald's class.

✔ Discuss Gerald's views on the working class and 'Daisy Renton'.

✔ Think about Priestley's views on the class divide.

✔ Use quotations to support your points.

✔ Analyse the effect of language.

Who, or what, is Eva Smith?

Assessment objectives
* AO1, AO2, AO3

Text references
You will have read from:
* the start of Act Two, to where the Inspector says: 'No. It wasn't necessary and I thought it better not to.'

What does Eva Smith represent?

Priestley uses the characters in *An Inspector Calls* as devices through which to explore social and political issues.

Eva Smith or Daisy Renton?

The name 'Eva' originates from Eve, who, according to Christian belief, was the first woman created and the one who led Adam into sin by eating the forbidden fruit. At the time Priestley wrote *An Inspector Calls*, 'Smith' was the most common surname in England.

1 Note down why you think Priestley chose the name 'Eva Smith'.

In the play, Eva Smith changes her name to Daisy Renton and, towards the end of Act Two, the audience learns that she also used other names. Gerald says 'she wanted to be Daisy Renton – and not Eva Smith'.

2 Discuss with a partner why you think Priestley chose to show Eva having more than one name. Consider:

* why she might not have wanted to be Eva Smith
* the significance of her appearing as more than one person.

Eva as working class

Eva's experiences exemplify Priestley's criticisms of the class divide, both in 1912 and in 1944.

3 Copy and complete the table below, considering the issues that Eva represents and what the play suggests about Priestley's opinion on the topic.

Issues faced by the working class	Quotation	Priestley's opinion and how we know
They were kept in their class by not being able to interact equally with – and in this case marry – people above their class.	'She knew it couldn't last – hadn't expected it to last.'	He thinks the working class are as good as the middle and upper classes, as he shows Eva's behaviour as good (e.g. saving money), while the behaviour of the middle and upper classes is not good.
	'Old Joe Meggarty, half-drunk and goggle-eyed, had wedged her into a corner with that obscene fat carcass of his.'	

	'... she was desperately hard up and at that moment was actually hungry.'	
	'And you used the power you had, as a daughter of a good customer and also of a man well known in the town, to punish the girl.'	
	'I told the girl to clear out and she went.'	

Eva as a woman

During the Second World War, gender equality and women's rights came to the fore, as women performed many traditionally 'male' jobs. Although women had many more rights in 1944 than they had in 1912, they were still not equal with men. Priestley explores these issues in *An Inspector Calls*.

4 Consider the issues facing women that Priestley raises through the character of Eva. Record these issues and Priestley's views on them in a table, like the one you completed in Task 3. Consider the following:

- sexual freedom
- wages
- financial independence
- working rights
- politics.

5 Now consider Sheila's life. As an upper-middle-class woman, does she face the same issues as Eva?

6 Eva Smith does not have any lines in the play. What can you infer from the absence of her voice?

Final task

7 Write three paragraphs explaining how Priestley uses Eva Smith as a device to explore *either* class *or* gender.

Checklist for success

✔ Describe Eva's experiences.
✔ Analyse the effect of Priestley's language choices in showing how she is treated.
✔ Use quotations to support your points.
✔ Explain what you think Eva's purpose is in the play – what does she symbolise?

Paper 2 Question 3: Use of language

Assessment objective
• AO2

> ## How can I write about the effect of language in a non-fiction text?

Paper 2 Question 3 is similar to Paper 1 Question 2. However, the section will be longer and there are no bullet points to support you. You will still get marks for the following:

- textual detail
- subject terminology
- the effects of language choices.

Parts of speech

You can use subject terminology by correctly identifying parts of speech.

1 Copy the sentences below and label each of the bold words with the correct part of speech: noun, adjective, adverb or verb.

   a '**Run** along.'

   b 'But these girls aren't **cheap labour** – they're **people**.'

   c 'You're **squiffy**.'

   d 'Though **naturally** I don't know anything about this **girl**.'

Textual detail

You must select the language choices made by the writer. These can be individual words, or devices such as similes.

2 Read the question and text below, selecting relevant and effective textual detail.

How does the writer use language to present the woman?

This extract is from a memoir where the writer recalls time spent living with the desperately poor in Paris and London. Here, he and a fellow tramp visit a woman who gives homeless people tea and a bun as long as they pray afterwards.

> Presently the door opened and a lady in a blue silk dress, wearing gold spectacles and a crucifix, welcomed us in. Inside were thirty or forty hard chairs, a harmonium and a very gory lithograph of the Crucifixion.
>
> Uncomfortably we took off our caps and sat down. The lady handed out the tea, and while we ate and drank, she moved to and fro, talking benignly. She talked upon religious subjects – about Jesus Christ always having a soft spot for poor rough men like us, and about how quickly the time passed when you were in church, and what a difference it made to a man on the road if he said his prayers regularly.

We hated it. We sat against the wall fingering our caps (a tramp feels indecently exposed with his cap off), and turning pink and trying to mumble something when the lady addressed us. There was no doubt that she meant it all kindly.

From *Down and Out in Paris and London* by George Orwell, 1933

The effect of language

When writing about the effect of language, you need to explain the connotations of the words or devices.

3 Choose four pieces of language that you selected from the extract. Copy and complete the table to show their effect.

Textual detail	Effect of language		
	What you think	**What you feel**	**What you imagine**
'silk'	She cares about her appearance. She has wealth.	Uncomfortable about the difference between the very poor men and her wealth.	An attractive, flowing dress that is soft and contrasts with the tramps' clothing.

Writing about the **cumulative** effect of language will help you reach the higher levels of the mark scheme. To do this, you should group two or more language choices that have a similar or cumulative effect.

4 Look again at the text and try to find language features whose effect adds to those you have already identified.

Key term

cumulative: referring to something that is added to several times to build it up in terms of size or effect

Final task

5 In 15 minutes, write a four-paragraph response to this question:
How does the writer use language to present the woman?

Literature link

The poverty shown in this extract is similar to the kind of poverty that Eva Smith and people like her would have faced. The support offered by the woman would have been quite common at the time and shows the sort of help that Mrs Birling's charity was supposed to offer.

Checklist for success

✔ Use textual detail/quotes.
✔ Use accurate subject terminology.
✔ Explore the effect of individual words and devices.
✔ Comment on the cumulative effect of language choices.

Paper 2 Question 4: Viewpoint

Assessment objective
• AO3

How can I read and plan for a comparison question?

Ideas and perspectives

Paper 2 Question 4 of your English Language exam will ask you to compare the views and perspectives of two writers on a particular topic. The question will look like this:

> For this question you should refer to **both** Source A and Source B.
>
> Compare how the two writers convey their different perspectives on women.
>
> In your answer you should:
>
> • compare their perspectives about women
> • compare the methods the writers use to convey their perspectives
> • support your ideas with quotations from both texts.

The topic of this question is women. In your answer, it is important that you write about the *writers' views and perspectives on women*, not just the topic of women.

1 Read the **topic sentences** below and decide if they clearly focus on the writers' ideas and perspectives of women, or whether they just focus on the topic of women.

- In Source A, the writer presents the idea that women should be educated but not partake in politics.
- In Source A, women are presented as not equal.
- In Source A, women are presented as having an important role to play in society.
- In Source A, the writer thinks that women should not strive for equality with men.
- In Source A, the writer believes that women striving for equality is vain.
- In Source A, women and men's responsibilities are different.
- In Source A, the writer's perspective is that women being involved in politics would damage the role they play in society.

Key term

topic sentence: the sentence that summarises what a paragraph is about; it is usually (although not always) the first sentence in a paragraph

The following sentence starters may help you to ensure that you are writing about the writers' ideas and perspectives:

- *The writer thinks/feels/believes …*

- *The writer introduces/presents/explores the idea that …*

2 Read Source A and Source B. Note down the main ideas and perspectives about women in each source.

Source A

A letter sent to a magazine and published in 1889.

An Appeal Against Female Suffrage

We, the undersigned, wish to appeal to the common sense and educated thought of the men and women of England against the proposed extension of the Parliamentary suffrage to women.

While desiring the fullest possible development of the powers, energies, and education of women, we believe that their work for the State, and their responsibilities towards it, must always differ essentially from those of men, and that therefore their share in the working of the State machinery should be different from that assigned to men. […] To men belong the struggle of debate and legislation in Parliament; the hard and exhausting labour implied in the administration of the national resources and powers; the conduct of England's relations towards the external world; the working of the army and navy; […] In all these spheres women's direct participation is made impossible either by the disabilities of sex, or by strong formations of custom and habit resting ultimately on physical difference, against which it is useless to contend. […] In conclusion: nothing can be further from our minds than to seek to depreciate the position or the importance of women. It is because we are keenly alive to the enormous value of their special contribution to the community, that we oppose what seems to us likely to endanger that contribution. We are convinced that the pursuit of a mere outward equality with men is for women not only vain but […] leads to a total misconception of woman's true dignity and special mission.

From 'An Appeal Against Female Suffrage', by Mrs Humphrey Ward, published in *The Nineteenth Century Magazine*, 1889

Source B

A magazine article written for a women's rights newspaper in the early 1900s.

Why I want the vote

I want the Vote because Lord Curzon says 'it is the imperishable heritage of the human race', and therefore it belongs to me.

I want it because the young workmen over the age of twenty-one whom I employ are going to the polls to proudly register their views on the Budget and Tariff Reform, while I, a middle-aged woman, sit in my office and construct the means by which they earn their living, yet am shut out myself.

I want it because I do not see why the women I employ – skilled workers, the chief or sole supporters of their humble homes – should not, the same as men, protect their labour and their other interests at the polls. I want the vote because I pay to educate the children of my older workmen, yet they, who pay no rates or taxes, are marching to the ballot-box, and the Government, which impudently robs me of my hard-earned money, would send me to prison as a third-class criminal were I to walk to St Stephen's and importune for a hearing to redress my grievances.

I want the Vote because Mr Lloyd George received a deputation of footballers who, in order to protect their playgrounds, claimed exemption from the land taxes in the proposed Budget; yet deputations of women desperately claiming protection for their livelihood and lives are derided and declined a hearing!

I want it because of the ever-increasing numbers of poor women who are annually murdered in this country, and because of the horrible apathy with which Parliament and Society meet the wholesale destruction of these girls.

[…]

I want the authority, which my responsibility as an experienced, thinking, intelligent member of the community demands, to reconstruct the false and cruel standard of morality by which forlorn maternity is so often plunged in the mire, and in its fear and frenzy driven to kill the thing it loves and longs for, namely, its young.

I want it for woman's work – to educate children, house the poor, protect the mother spirit, to vote away the bad divorce law which the 'Englishman's sense of fair play' has thought good enough for English wives! Lady McLaren's Charter would, at one fell stroke, uproot the many wrongs from which our women suffer; but who to force that Charter home without the weapon of the Vote? Impossible! – and that is why I want it!

From 'Why I Want the Vote' by Maude Arncliffe-Sennett,
published in *The Vote*, 1910

Collecting views and perspectives for your answer

In order to complete a question like Task 2 above, you need to be aware of the *views* expressed and the *language* used in both sources. Remember that, in the exam, you would have already summarised a topic from both sources and have analysed the language from a section of one of them.

 3 The sort of notes that you might already have written on the content of Source A are provided below. Copy the table and complete the notes for Source B. Remember to be systematic. Read the text line by line and ask yourself: 'Is this showing a perspective?'

Source A	Source B
Positive about women – women have dignity.	
Positive about women – women have a special position.	
Positive about women – women have an enormous role in society.	
Positive about women – women make a special contribution to society.	
Women should not have the right to vote.	
Women are 'disabled' by their sex.	
Women are 'disabled' by the customs and habits of society.	
Being involved in debate/legislation will endanger women's other roles.	
Being involved in administration of the country is very hard work – implication is women are not strong enough.	

When you have completed the notes for Source B, draw a line to join related points between Source A and Source B. If they are the same, then use a blue pen; if they are different or contrasting, use a red pen.

Now select two or three things to compare; they can be similarities or differences. Once you have decided on the comparisons you are going to make, you will need to choose quotations to support your points.

4 Find quotations to support your selected comparisons. Remember –
you need quotations to support your points about *both* texts.

Collecting language features for your answer

There are no marks for comparing the methods the writers have used or
their effect. However, you do need to include writers' methods and how
they convey perspective. If you do not include writers' methods, you will
be limited to half marks (8 out of 16).

You do not need to refer directly to the reader, as the mark scheme does
not focus on readers' interpretations. You are required to focus on the
views of the writer and the methods they use to show those views. To do
this, you should select either individual words or language devices that
you think are effective in conveying the writer's perspective. For example:

an adverb that indicates that the men are
very aware and feel it intensely, again trying to
show that they value women's roles

... we are keenly alive to the enormous value
of their special contribution to the community ...

a vague noun – illustrates that
they offer positives but they're not
specific (like jobs are for men)

a patronising adjective – trying to make
women sound important and valued

5 Read your selected quotations. Then annotate them to
highlight the words or language devices that convey the writer's
perspective and show how they do so.

Your comparative introduction

Before you write your main paragraphs, write an outline of the different
overall viewpoints of the writers. In this case, this summary would state
that one source advocates women having the vote, while the other one
opposes female suffrage.

6 Write your introduction.

Writing your comparison

Once you have completed your notes, you can write your answer. You
will get marks for the following:

- ideas and perspectives of the writers
- textual detail
- writers' methods and their effects
- comparison of viewpoints and methods.

Look at the example below. Note how it finds both a broad similarity, shown by the word 'both', and a specific difference.

Both of these sources consider the role of women in society and both say positive things about women. Source A suggests that they are of 'enormous value', whilst Source B is more specific when she describes herself as 'experienced, thinking, intelligent'. Notably, the first source uses a very vague noun to convey what is positive about women, referring only to their 'value'. This contrasts significantly with Source B's author, who uses a list of adjectives, outlining the skills of women. She uses the present participle 'thinking' to indicate that women are intellectually able and that they consider things carefully and at length. Source A's author views women in terms of what they can offer as 'value' rather than what they deserve in return, while the author of Source B believes their qualities mean they deserve something in return: the vote.

7 Identify where this example response fulfils the bullet-point list above.

Final task

8 Write two more paragraphs about the similarities and contrasts in the content and language of the two sources. You could consider what they say about women's strengths and weaknesses.

Checklist for success

✔ Include statements about the ideas and perspectives of the writers.

✔ Support your points with textual detail.

✔ Analyse the effect of writers' methods.

✔ Compare the viewpoints of the writers.

Literature link

These pieces of writing show the debates about women and their role in society which were raging throughout Eva's and Sheila's lifetime. They help us to see how Sheila is struggling to find authority in a new world for women. They enable us to understand what Eva was trying to do with her life and the restrictions placed upon her by society.

End of chapter task

1 Gerald's character is developed further in Act Three, but already, at the end of Act Two, we feel we have an understanding of him and his feelings. Use your knowledge of Acts One and Two and your notes about Gerald to answer the following question.

How does Priestley present Gerald in Acts One and Two of *An Inspector Calls*? Write about:

- what Gerald says and does in Acts One and Two of *An Inspector Calls*
- how Priestley presents Gerald by the ways he writes.

Check your progress

- I can write clearly about the characters in their society.
- I can clearly explain how Priestley's methods create character.
- I can show clear understanding of society in Britain in 1912.

- I can write critically about the characters in their society.
- I can analyse the ways in which Priestley's methods create character.
- I can show thoughtful consideration of society in Britain in 1912.

Chapter 6

Act Two: The climax of the play

English Literature

You will read:

- Act Two, from Gerald's exit to the end of the act.

You will explore:

- Mrs Birling's role in the play
- the methods Priestley uses to create tension
- how Priestley presents women in the play.

English Language

You will read:

- an extract from a short story from 1894 by Kate Chopin about a recently widowed woman.

You will explore:

- how writers use structure to achieve effects and influence readers.

Impressions of Mrs Birling

Assessment objectives
- AO1, AO2

Text references
You will have read from:
- Gerald's exit to the end of Act Two.

How does Priestley undermine the views of Mrs Birling?

First impressions of Mrs Birling

At the beginning of the play, Priestley uses the stage directions and dialogue as **exposition** about Mrs Birling's character. This helps the audience to understand her social status and personality. For example:

> 'His wife is about fifty, a rather cold woman and her husband's social superior.'

Key term

exposition: the giving of information about a character, setting or event

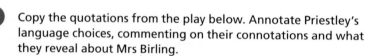

lacking in feeling and kindness; formal to the point of appearing aloof

more important and with more status; more money and higher class; better spoken

1 Copy the quotations from the play below. Annotate Priestley's language choices, commenting on their connotations and what they reveal about Mrs Birling.

> '(*Reproachfully*) Arthur, you're not supposed to say such things –'
>
> 'When you're married you'll realise that men with important work to do sometimes have to spend nearly all their energy on their business.'
>
> 'Now stop it, you two.'

Mrs Birling's status

Mrs Birling's social status means she is used to having control of a situation. When her authority and morals are challenged by Inspector Goole, she responds with defiance.

2 Reread Mrs Birling's speech to the Inspector that begins, 'If you think you can bring pressure to bear upon me …'

What does this statement reveal about how she regards her own status?

Mrs Birling has very clear views about class. She believes that her social standing makes her morally superior to those of a lower class.

3   **a**   Find three quotations from Mrs Birling's speech that are evidence of her view that she is morally superior.

      b   For each quotation, note down what it suggests about her view of the working class.

      c   Are her views similar to those of other characters in the play?

Mrs Birling as a woman of charity

Mrs Birling is the chair of the Brumley Women's Charity Organisation. Inspector Goole asks if it is an organisation which supports 'women in distress'.

4   Consider Mrs Birling's response and how she later refuses to support Eva Smith. What kind of criteria do you think Mrs Birling used to decide whether to give or refuse support to the women who came to her?

Mrs Birling's refusal to support Eva Smith ultimately results in the young woman's death.

5   In pairs, discuss what alternative there may be to such charity guided by moralistic judgements. What might Priestley have been looking forward to? Look back at Lesson 1.3 to remind yourself about the social changes being introduced at the time he was writing the play, if you need to.

Mrs Birling's loss of control

When Mrs Birling finally realises that the father of Eva's child – whom she has been blaming for Eva's death – is Eric, the stage directions show a distinct change in her. She moves from speaking 'triumphantly' to being speechless and 'frightened'.

6   Look at the **juxtaposition** in the way Mrs Birling speaks at the start of this section and at the end. Write a short explanation of why you think Priestley uses this device of contrasting. How does it make the audience feel towards her?

> **Key term**
>
> **juxtaposition:** placing two contrasting things or ideas together for effect, usually to emphasise their differences

Final task

7   Write two paragraphs in response to the following question:

How does Priestley present Mrs Birling in the play?

You may wish to consider:

- how Mrs Birling is established by Priestley
- what views Mrs Birling represents
- how and why Priestley makes her character unlikeable.

Developing tension towards the play's climax

Assessment objectives
• AO1, AO2

Text references
You will have read from:
• where Mrs Birling says, 'You have a photograph of this girl?' to the end of Act Two.

How does Priestley develop the tension in Act Two?

The end of the rising action and the climax

The end of Act Two is very tense, both for the characters and the audience, as the narrative leads towards its climax.

1 Look again at the end of Act Two. Return to the narrative arc you drew in Lesson 4.1 and label the key events that contribute to the tension at the end of the rising action and then the climax at the end of the act.

Developing tension

Towards the end of Act Two, Priestley uses four key methods to create tension as the play builds to its climax:

• dramatic irony about Eric
• Sheila's warnings to Mrs Birling
• the Inspector's confident speeches
• Mrs Birling's defiant responses.

2 Look at the quotations below. Match each one to one of the tension-creating methods listed above.

a	'(*sternly*) I warn you, you're making it worse for yourself.'
b	'You're quite wrong to suppose I shall regret what I did.'
c	'I accept no blame for it at all.'
d	'I blame the young man who was the father of the child she was going to have.'
e	'If, as she said, he didn't belong to her class, and was some drunken young idler, then that's all the more reason why he shouldn't escape.'
f	'Then he'd be entirely responsible.'
g	'Certainly. And he ought to be dealt with very severely —'
h	'(*with sudden alarm*) Mother – stop – stop!'
i	'Don't worry, Mrs Birling. I shall do my duty.'
j	'No hushing up, eh? Make an example of the young man, eh?'
k	'I consider it your duty. And now, no doubt, you'd like to say good night.'
l	'(*distressed*) Now, Mother – don't you see?'

Select one example of each method and discuss with a partner why you think it adds to the tension.

Focusing on the language

Priestley also uses a range of language and structural devices to help develop the tension:

- **interrogatives**
- dashes or pauses
- adjectives
- adverbs
- repetition
- exclamation marks
- **fragments**
- simple sentences.

You have looked at some of the lines that build the tension in this part of the play. Focusing on language and structure will help you explore the devices Priestley uses to create this tension. For example:

> **Key terms**
>
> **interrogative:** a question word (e.g. how, when, why)
>
> **fragment:** groups of words that are not proper sentences

the adjective/past participle shows Sheila has realised the truth and is very upset, showing how dramatic and severe the situation is

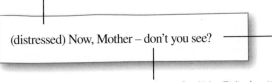

(distressed) Now, Mother – don't you see?

the interrogative highlights the dramatic irony and creates tension as the audience waits for Mrs Birling to realise

the pause builds tension as the audience (and Mrs Birling) wait to see what Sheila is going to say – it could be her composing herself after her realisation

 a Write out one of your quotations from Task 3. Underline and label the language choices that help to build the tension.

b Share your annotations with a partner and discuss how you think the quotation you have chosen adds to the tension. Expand your annotations to explain this.

> **Checklist for success**
>
> ✔ Identify a device that creates tension.
> ✔ Support your point with a quotation.
> ✔ Explain how the device creates tension.

Final task

 Write two paragraphs explaining how Priestley creates tension in the lead-up to the climax of the play.

Women in the play

Assessment objectives
- AO1, AO2, AO3

Text references
You will read:
- up to the end of Act Two.

How does Priestley present the role of women in *An Inspector Calls*?

Context: the roles of women in 1912 and 1944

The position of women changed quite significantly between 1912 and 1944, when Priestley wrote *An Inspector Calls*. By 1944, women had the same voting rights as men and divorce laws were fairer to women. Their roles had also broadened.

 Draw up a list of contextual points you can remember about women and their roles in 1912 and 1944. Make a separate list for each time period.

Sheila and Mrs Birling

Sheila and Mrs Birling have very different views about how women should behave and how they should be treated. Mrs Birling represents a traditional 1912 role. Sheila's views are more progressive for the time, and may reflect some of the challenges to traditional thinking that were occurring in the suffragette movement.

 Copy the table below. For each point about the role of women, consider the difference in attitude and behaviour between Sheila and Mrs Birling. In the character columns, add a quotation or reference to an event. In the 'Contrast' column, note the difference between the characters and why you think Priestley used this contrast.

Role of women	Sheila	Mrs Birling	Contrast
Questioning their husband/fiancé			
Relationship with their husband/fiancé			
Using improper language			
Expressing their opinion			
Being exposed to unpleasant things			

 Although Mrs Birling fulfils the more traditional role of a woman in many respects, she repeatedly challenges the men, particularly Inspector Goole and her husband. Discuss with a partner what this reveals about Mrs Birling's world view. What is more important as a determiner of her role: her sex or her class?

An aesthetic view of women

'Aesthetic' is an adjective that means 'concerned with beauty'. All the men in *An Inspector Calls* refer to Eva Smith through the lens of her aesthetics. Even Sheila asks whether Eva was 'pretty'.

The Inspector: 'she had been pretty – very pretty.'

Mr Birling: 'She was a lively, good looking girl.'

Gerald: 'She was very pretty – soft brown hair and big dark eyes.'

Eric: 'she was pretty and a good sport.'

4 Discuss with a partner what the implication of this **motif** is. What might Priestley be hinting at?

Mr Birling expresses views on women that both his 1944 audience and an audience today would consider **stereotypical** and demeaning:

> '... clothes mean something quite different to a woman. Not just something to wear – and not only something to make 'em look prettier – but – well, a sort of sign or token of their self-respect.'

5 Note down what you think this comment reveals about Birling's attitude to women and what he considers their value to be. What assumptions does he make?

The role of women in the play

Priestley explores the varying roles of women through Sheila, Eva and Mrs Birling. Asking questions about *why* things happen to the women in the play can help you understand Priestley's motivations and the ideas he wanted to convey to his audience.

6 Write a short explanation for each of the following questions:

a Why does Priestley make the younger character, Sheila, different from Mrs Birling?

b Why does Priestley show a significant change in Sheila through the play?

c Why does Eva, who perhaps has the most important role in the play, never get the opportunity to speak?

Final task

7 How does Priestley present the role of women in Acts One and Two of *An Inspector Calls*? Write about:

- the roles women take in the play
- how Priestley presents women and the language he uses.

Checklist for success
....

✔ Refer to both the 1912 and 1944 contexts.

✔ Refer to events in the play and how they explore the role of women.

✔ Use quotations to support your points.

✔ Clearly explain what you believe to be Priestley's views.

✔ Explore an aspect of language that Priestley uses to communicate these ideas.

Paper 1 Question 3: The effects of structure

Assessment objective
• AO2

How can I write about the effects of structure?

What is structure?

Paper 1 Question 3 will ask you to write about the effects of structure. For this, you need to focus on the **sequencing** of the text and the effect this has on the reader.

Key term

sequencing: ordering

 Match the following structural features with the correct definition from the box below.

a   change of focus

b   overview

c   pivotal moment

d   sequence

e   deductive description

f   inductive description

g   foregrounding

1	Moving from one character, place or theme to another
2	A summary of the overall important features
3	An important event that marks a change in tone or narrative direction
4	The order of the text
5	Describing a zoomed-out scene
6	Describing a zoomed-in scene
7	Placing something in focus so that it is the most prominent or important feature
8	Indicating a future event

Approaching the structure question

The question will ask you to analyse the effects of the structure across the whole extract. It will look something like this:

> **You now need to think about the whole of the source. This text is taken from near the end of a short story. How has the writer structured the text to interest you as a reader?**
>
> You could write about:
> - what the writer focuses your attention on at the beginning
> - how and why the writer changes this focus as the source develops
> - any other structural features that interest you.

You will need to include subject terminology, textual detail and effect. However, the most important thing is to show a clear understanding of how the order of the text works as a whole and what effect that has on the reader.

The first step is to read the text paragraph by paragraph, noting down what the writer focuses attention on in each paragraph.

 Read the source below and make notes about the focus of each paragraph.

In the following extract from Kate Chopin's 'The Story of an Hour' Mrs Mallard has been told that her husband has died in a railway disaster. The reader is also told at the outset that Mrs Mallard has 'heart trouble'. The scene below shows Mrs Mallard as she retires to her bedroom, refusing company, exhausted after 'a storm of grief'.

There stood, facing the open window, a comfortable, roomy armchair. Into this she sank, pressed down by a physical exhaustion that haunted her body and seemed to reach into her soul.

She could see in the open square before her house the tops of trees that were all aquiver with the new spring life. The delicious breath of rain was in the air. In the street below a peddler was crying his wares. The notes of a distant song which someone was singing reached her faintly, and countless sparrows were twittering in the eaves.

There were patches of blue sky showing here and there through the clouds that had met and piled one above the other in the west facing her window.

She sat with her head thrown back upon the cushion of the chair, quite motionless, except when a sob came up into her throat and shook her, as a child who has cried itself to sleep continues to sob in its dreams.

She was young, with a fair, calm face, whose lines bespoke repression and even a certain strength. But now there was a dull stare in her eyes, whose gaze was fixed away off yonder on one of those patches of blue sky. It was not a glance of reflection, but rather indicated a suspension of intelligent thought.

There was something coming to her and she was waiting for it, fearfully. What was it? She did not know; it was too subtle and elusive to name. But she felt it, creeping out of the sky, reaching toward her through the sounds, the scents, the color that filled the air.

Now her bosom rose and fell tumultuously. She was beginning to recognize this thing that was approaching to possess her, and she was striving to beat it back with her will – as powerless as her two white slender hands would have been. When she abandoned herself a little whispered word escaped her slightly parted lips. She said it over and over under her breath: 'free, free, free!' The vacant stare and the look of terror that had followed it went from her eyes. They stayed keen and bright. Her pulses beat fast, and the coursing blood warmed and relaxed every inch of her body.

She did not stop to ask if it were or were not a monstrous joy that held her. A clear and exalted perception enabled her to dismiss the suggestion as trivial. She knew that she would weep again when she saw the kind, tender hands folded in death; the face that had never looked save with love upon her, fixed and gray and dead. But she saw beyond that bitter moment a long procession of years to come that would belong to her absolutely. And she opened and spread her arms out to them in welcome.

There would be no one to live for during those coming years; she would live for herself. There would be no powerful will bending hers in that blind persistence with which men and women believe they have a right to impose a private will upon a fellow-creature. A kind intention or a cruel intention made the act seem no less a crime as she looked upon it in that brief moment of illumination.

And yet she had loved him – sometimes. Often she had not. What did it matter! What could love, the unsolved mystery, count for in the face of this possession of self-assertion which she suddenly recognized as the strongest impulse of her being!

'Free! Body and soul free!' she kept whispering.

From 'The Story of an Hour' by Kate Chopin, 1894

The next step is to focus on the effect that the structure has on the reader.

 Note down what you think, feel and imagine as you read each paragraph. Use a different colour pen for each.

An overview of the source

It is wise to begin your writing with an overview of the whole extract, considering how the action or tension progresses. Do not just retell the story; you should explain how the reader responds to the text as a whole and any developments in it.

 Write a brief overview of what happens and your reaction to it as a reader. Consider the following points:

- the initial establishment of the woman's grief
- the shock of her feeling 'free'
- the growing celebration at his death.

Literature link

This text shows how women's lives were controlled by their husbands and how wives had to bend to husbands' wills – much as Mrs Birling tells Sheila that women have to get used to their husbands spending all their time and energy on business.

Planning your analysis

Now you need to select two or three factors to focus on in more detail. It is likely that you will include at least one point from your overview.

5 Which of the structural devices below are used effectively in the source? Label them. Add any others you can find.

- change of focus
- pivotal moment
- sequencing
- foregrounding.

In the exam you will only have time to write your plan in note form. However, when practising, it can be helpful to plan in more detail to make writing your response easier.

6 Copy and complete the chart below as a plan for a response to the question.

Structural device	Quotation	Effect (what you think, feel, imagine)	Why it matters that it is placed where it is
Sequencing – there's a hint that something is wrong at the beginning.	'pressed down by a physical exhaustion that haunted her body'	It makes me question what is wrong with her and why she is so tired and 'haunted'. I feel concerned for her.	It is placed at the start so that the reader knows something is wrong, which develops tension, especially when it is then not explained and the focus turns to the scene – so it remains unexplained.

Final task

 7 Turn your plan into a written response. Spend no more than 12 minutes on it.

Checklist for success

✔ Give an overview of the text as a whole.
✔ Write two or three additional paragraphs about a particular structural device.
✔ Support your points with short quotations.
✔ Explain the effect of the device and why it is placed where it is.

End of chapter task

1 Use your knowledge of Mrs Birling from reading the play so far, and any notes you have made in this chapter, to answer the following question.

How does Priestley use Mrs Birling to present the theme of class in Act One and Act Two of *An Inspector Calls*? Write about:

- ideas about class in the play
- how Priestley presents class through what Mrs Birling says and does.

Check your progress

- I can write clearly about ideas in the play.
- I can clearly explain how Priestley's methods explore ideas.
- I can show clear understanding of the contextual factors that influenced Priestley's writing.

- I can write critically about ideas in the play.
- I can analyse the ways Priestley's methods explore ideas.
- I can show thoughtful consideration of the contextual factors that influenced Priestley's writing.

Act Three:
The falling action

English Literature

You will read:

- the whole of Act Three.

You will explore:

- how themes can be investigated through characters
- the theme of repentance in *An Inspector Calls*
- the effect of the play's ending.

English Language

You will read:

- an example of a viewpoint question.

You will explore:

- how to develop ideas with rhetorical devices in point-of-view writing.

Understanding Eric

Assessment objectives
• AO1, AO2, AO3

Text references
You will have read from:
• the beginning of Act Three to the end of the play.

What is the function of the character Eric in *An Inspector Calls*?

Foreshadowing

At the beginning of the play, Priestley uses **foreshadowing** to hint at what the audience later learns about Eric: he drinks too much; he disagrees with his father's world view; he is secretly involved with women; and he has something to hide.

> **Key term**
>
> **foreshadowing:** a warning or an indication of a future event

1 Look at the following quotations from the start of Act One. Note down which later event or revelation Priestley is foreshadowing.

  a 'You're squiffy.'

  b 'Yes, I know – but still –'

  c '(*eagerly*) Yes, I remember – (*but he checks himself*)'

  d '(*who is uneasy, sharply*) Here, what do you mean?'

Eric's relationship with his parents

The foreshadowing hints at Eric's character and actions, so the audience becomes suspicious of him quite early in the play. However, the later revelations about him come as a complete surprise to Mr and Mrs Birling.

2 Discuss with a partner what you think their surprise shows about Eric's relationship with his parents.

Throughout the play, Eric comes into conflict with both his parents. Mr Birling contradicts him and Mrs Birling tells him off. During Mr Birling's speech in Act One, Eric interrupts and asks him, 'What about war?' and Birling declares, 'there isn't a chance of war'.

3 The audience in 1944 – and an audience today – would of course know that war did follow. Write a short explanation of what this makes you think about Eric and about the way his father reacts to him.

Eric's values are clearly different from Mr Birling's. Eric complains about how the family money is earned (although he still benefits from the profits). Mrs Birling says, 'Your trouble is you've been spoilt.'

4 Consider Eric's behaviour throughout the play. What evidence can you find that he is spoilt? Use quotations to back up your points.

When Eric admits what happened with Eva and confesses to stealing from the factory, Mr Birling asks him why he did not come to him for help. Eric replies: 'Because you're not the kind of father a chap could go to when he's in trouble – that's why.' Later, he also says that Mrs Birling is not understanding: 'You don't understand anything. You never did. You never even tried –'

 5   Write a paragraph that summarises how you think Eric felt about his parents before Inspector Goole arrived. Then write a second paragraph that summarises how you think he felt after Inspector Goole arrived and told them about Eva Smith.

Eric's sense of responsibility

After Inspector Goole arrives, Priestley creates a distinct contrast between Eric and Mr Birling. When Eric learns about Eva's death, he responds dramatically: '*(involuntarily)* My God!'

 6   Write a paragraph that explains what Eric's reaction shows the audience about how he views the working class. How does this differ from the views or reactions of other characters? Why do you think this may be his view?

Priestley juxtaposes Mr Birling and Eric's views about employers' responsibilities early on in the play, giving Eric a more sympathetic view of the working class than his father. Despite this, Eric continues to live from his father's wealth, despite professing to dislike the values that generate it.

 7   Debate with a partner whether you think Eric is a hypocrite and why.

 8   **a** Read the quotations below and select any language choices that you think effectively portray Eric's sense of social responsibility, his tone and his attitude. Consider Priestley's use of personal pronouns, verbs and adjectives.

'It isn't if you can't go and work somewhere else.'

'He could have kept her on instead of throwing her out. I call it tough luck.'

'Well, I think it's a dam' shame ... I'd have let her stay.'

      b Note down their connotations and the effects of the words you have selected. What do they reveal about Eric's views? What do they make the audience think, feel or imagine?

Eric's attitude towards personal responsibility also contrasts with that of Mr Birling. From the first mention of Eva's death he has a clear sense of the consequence of actions: 'Is that why she committed suicide? When was this, Father?' Later, when he finds out that his father sacked her, he says: 'That might have started it.'

 9   Consider what Eric says about his relationship with Eva. Note down how he attempted to show responsibility to her and the child.

The audience understands that Eric is a well-educated young man. Mr Birling refers to his 'varsity' life, referring to university (probably Oxford or Cambridge).

10 Why do you think that Priestley chose to give an educated character more socialist views?

Eric and Eva

Eric conflicts with Mr and Mrs Birling – both unlikeable characters. But despite this, and his more sympathetic views of the working class, he also exhibits behaviour that makes him difficult to like. By the end of the play, Eric has repented of his actions, but Priestley still presents this character as deeply flawed.

11 Draw up a list of actions that give the audience a negative view of Eric.

12 Copy the following quotation, in which Eric admits what he did to Eva Smith. Annotate it, focusing on what makes the act so horrible and such an abuse of power.

> 'Yes, I insisted – it seems. I'm not very clear about it, but afterwards she told me she didn't want to go in but that – well, I was in that state when a chap easily turns nasty – and I threatened to make a row.'

13 Discuss with a partner why Priestley may have chosen to present Eric in this way. Consider the following questions:

- What point was Priestley trying to make?
- What was he saying about young middle-class men of that time? How did they treat working-class women?
- Is it important that Eric wants to be different from his father?

Repentance and blame

Eric is clearly repentant for his behaviour and understands that the worst of his actions are the ones that harmed another human being:

'(*shouting*) And I say the girl's dead and we all helped to kill her – and that's what matters –'

14 How does Priestley use language in this quotation to show that Eric is sincerely sorry?

At the end of the play, both Eric and Sheila speak as if they are now committed to social responsibility. Even when they realise that the whole thing was a hoax, Eric still dislikes the way his parents behave and talk: 'I agree with Sheila. It frightens me too.'

Eric places the blame for Eva's death with Mrs Birling, because she refused to give her financial help:

> 'Then – you killed her. She came to you to protect me – and you turned her away – yes, and you killed her – and the child she'd have too – my child – your own grandchild – you killed them both – damn you, damn you –'

15 Discuss with a partner whether you think this accusation is fair, and why.

16 Look at the language and devices Priestley uses in the quotation above. Note down how you think he has made the accusation more emotive. Use the following subject terminology to help you:

- personal pronouns
- dashes
- fragments
- emotive language
- **coordinating conjunctions**
- repetition
- aphorism.

Key terms

coordinating conjunction: a word that links two clauses of equal value in a sentence (e.g. and, but, or)

Final task

17 Priestley uses each of the characters in the play to explore different themes and ideas. What do you think is Eric's function in the play? What does he represent? Write two paragraphs explaining your ideas.

Checklist for success

✔ Comment on the contexts of both 1912 and 1944.
✔ Consider the key social and political ideas explored in the play.
✔ Use quotations to support your points.
✔ Explore the effects of language.

The theme of repentance

Assessment objectives
* AO1, AO2

Text references
You will have read from:
* the beginning of Act Three to the end of the play.

Why is repentance important in *An Inspector Calls?*

What is repentance?

Repentance is the act of being remorseful or very sorry.

1 Look at the quotations in the table below. Copy and complete the table by writing a sentence or two explaining how repentant each character is about their treatment of Eva Smith.

Character	Quotation	How repentant?
Mr Birling	'I can't accept any responsibility.'	
Sheila	'It's the only time I've ever done anything like that, and I'll never, never do it again to anybody.'	
Gerald	'She didn't blame me at all. I wish to God she had now. Perhaps I'd feel better about it.'	
Mrs Birling	'(*very distressed now*) No – Eric – please – I didn't know – I didn't understand –'	
Eric	'(*unhappily*) My God – I'm not likely to forget.'	

2 Write a short explanation of why you think Priestley shows two middle-class characters, Eric and Sheila, as sincerely repentant about the way they treated a working-class woman. What might he be trying to suggest to his audience?

The Inspector's response

Priestley contrasts Sheila's clear repentance with Mr and Mrs Birling's lack of it. As a result of her response, Inspector Goole treats Sheila and her parents differently.

3 Copy each of Inspector Goole's quotations below and note which character he is speaking to. Annotate each quotation with the tone the Inspector takes and what this reveals about his attitude towards the character he is speaking to.

a | '(Dryly) I don't play golf.'

b | 'The girl's dead though.'

c | '(Steadily) That's more or less what I was thinking earlier tonight, when I was in the Infirmary looking at what was left of Eva Smith. A nice little promising life there, I thought, and a nasty mess somebody's made of it.'

d	'Yes, I'm afraid it did.'
e	'you're partly to blame'
f	'(harshly) Yes, but you can't. It's too late. She's dead.'
g	'(very sternly) Her position now is that she lies with a burnt-out inside on a slab.'
h	'Don't stammer and yammer at me again.'
i	'(very deliberately) I think you did something terribly wrong – and that you're going to spend the rest of your life regretting it.'
j	'You made her pay a heavy price for that. And now she'll make you pay a heavier price still.'

4 For each quotation above, note down what Priestley might have been trying to convey to his audience. Link your notes to the idea of repentance where you can.

5 Look closely at the Inspector's behaviour towards Sheila. Compare this with the way he speaks to Mr and Mrs Birling. Discuss with a partner what you notice and why you think Priestley included this contrast.

How repentance affects the audience's view of character

Priestley uses the theme of repentance to help the audience reach a judgement about the characters in the play. Towards the end of Act Two, the Inspector says to Mrs Birling, 'You're not even sorry now, when you know what happened to the girl?'

6 Discuss with a partner how Priestley wants the audience to feel about Mr and Mrs Birling, compared with Sheila. Would the audience reaction be different if Sheila was not repentant or if Mr and Mrs Birling were?

Final task

7 Plan a response to the following exam-style question:

How does Priestley use his characters to explore the theme of repentance?
Write about:
- which characters are shown to be repentant
- how Priestley presents repentance through what his characters say and do.

You could use the following structure to help you plan for this theme question:
- Introduction: Answer the question and explain what Priestley is trying to say about the theme.
- Explain *where* Priestley first establishes the theme.
- Explain *where* Priestley explores the theme further.
- Explain *how* Priestley explores the theme in more depth.
- Explain *how* the theme is concluded in the play.
- Conclusion: Discuss what you think the audience might think and feel about the theme at the end.

Paper 2 Question 5: Writing to present a viewpoint

Assessment objectives
- AO5, AO6

How can I plan my writing to present a viewpoint?

Different forms and their features

Paper 2 Question 5 of your English Language exam will ask you to write in one of five different forms:

- letter
- article
- text for a leaflet
- text of a speech.
- essay

1 For each of the five forms, write a bullet-point list of the key features that you would need to use.

The question

The question will begin with a quotation about the topic you will be writing about. It will then give you a writing task that asks you to explain your point of view on the topic within one of the five forms. For example:

> 'School life is miserable for some students because so many people in school can be unkind. All students are responsible for the happiness of all others and they should try to be as kind as they can.'
>
> Write a speech aimed at Year 10 students in which you explain your point of view on this statement.

2 Read the question and identify which form you are being asked to write in.

In your response, you will need to fully explain your views on the topic. You might fully agree with the statement or fully disagree with it. Equally, you may agree with some parts of the statement and disagree with others.

3 Look at the quotation in the question and list your initial thoughts about the topic. Think carefully about whether you agree or disagree with the key parts of the statement.

Rhetorical devices

In point-of-view writing, **rhetorical devices** can help you to support your points. They should only be used where they build upon or prove your argument, so don't use too many; think about which ones will add the most weight to your argument. A useful way to remember rhetorical devices, so that your have a range at your disposal, is to use a mnemonic. 'PIRATE MOUSE' helps you to remember 11 different rhetorical devices.

Key terms

rhetorical device: a method of conveying a particular meaning or persuading the reader to agree with a particular point of view

mnemonic: a way of remembering something, such as using a pattern of letters or ideas

Letter	Device	Definition	Example
P	Pairs (contrasting)	Two contrasting examples used together	The popular and the lonely
I	Imperatives	Instructions to the reader	Change your school now.
R	Rhetorical questions	Questions designed to make the reader think	Don't you care about your fellow students?
A	Anecdote	Telling a story to illustrate your point	Yusef has experienced years of bullying. As a result, he …
T	Threes	Repeating a word or phrase three times	Students need support; they need friends; they need you.
E	Emotive language	Language designed to stir emotions in the reader	Children are needlessly dying after extreme bullying.
M	Modal verbs	Verbs that imply the future can be different	could, would, should, can, might
O	Opinions	Opinions of experts (scientists, legal groups, professionals, etc.)	The Department for Education states that bullying is more prevalent and more damaging now than it has ever been.
U	Personal pronoun	Addressing the reader directly	you, us, we
S	Statistics	The use of number facts	78% of gay students said they felt isolated by their peers.
E	Exaggeration	Making things more extreme than they are	Our school simply cannot continue this way.

4 Write 'PIRATE MOUSE' in the margin of your book and try to recall the rhetorical devices that each letter represents.

5 Reread the exam-style question above and note down the rhetorical devices you could use to express your opinions on the topic.

Final task

6 Plan and write your response to the question. Take no more than 45 minutes.

Checklist for success

✔ Write in paragraphs.
✔ Develop your argument clearly
✔ Use a variety of sentence structures.
✔ Use a range of vocabulary choices.
✔ Ensure you use a range of accurate punctuation.
✔ Include rhetorical devices.

The play's structure and ending

Assessment objectives
- AO1, AO2, AO3

Text references
You will have read from:
- the beginning of Act Three to the end of the play.

What is the importance of the ending of *An Inspector Calls*?

When is the climax of the play?

In Chapter 6, you looked at the ways in which Priestley built the tension to lead towards the climax at the end of Act Two.

1 Now that you have read the whole play, discuss with a partner whether you still think that the end of Act Two is the climax, or whether this occurs at a different point.

2 Return to the narrative arc that you began in Lesson 4.1 and continued in Lesson 6.2. Add labels for the key events alongside the key narrative features: exposition, catalyst, rising action, climax, falling action, resolution.

The falling action – character development

When Gerald returns to the Birlings' home and the family realise that Inspector Goole was not who he said he was, they react in very different ways.

3 Write a brief summary of the response of each character.

There is a real contrast between the emotions of Mr and Mrs Birling before and after they decide the Inspector's visit was a hoax.

4 Look at the stage directions used to describe the speech of these two characters before and after, then copy and complete the table below with the connotations of the language and what this reveals about the character's thoughts and feelings.

Character	Stage direction	Connotations from language	Character's thoughts and feelings
Mr Birling	*unhappily*		
Mr Birling	*angrily*		
Mr Birling	*triumphantly*		
Mr Birling	*amused*		
Mrs Birling	*distressed*		
Mrs Birling	*smiling*		

Sheila's speech changes more subtly before and after the family considers Inspector Goole's visit to be a hoax.

5 Look at the stage directions used to describe Sheila's speech, then copy and complete the table below with the connotations of the language and what this tells us about her thoughts and feelings.

Stage direction	Connotations from language	Sheila's thoughts and feelings
frightened		
scornfully		
tensely		
bitterly		

6 Using both tables, write a paragraph explaining what – if anything – you think the characters have learned from Inspector Goole's visit.

The surreal ending: who or what is the Inspector?

The surreal ending of the play has left many critics and audiences unsure of who or what Inspector Goole is. Many different interpretations try to explain what his character represents:

- He is a supernatural character, hence his name.
- He is the voice of God.
- He is the voice of conscience.
- He is a mouthpiece for Priestley's beliefs.
- He represents the consequences of actions.

7 Look at each of the suggestions above. In small groups, discuss which interpretation you agree with most. Try to use evidence from the text and the context to support your views and challenge the views of others.

8 The audience learns some key things about the characters' thoughts and feelings once Inspector Goole leaves. Write a list of the key things that the audience learns.

9 Discuss with a partner why you think Priestley did not just end the play after the Inspector leaves. Consider how this decision may have been influenced by the context of 1944, in which Priestley was writing, and the idea that Britain would have to change at the end of the Second World War.

Final task

10 What do you think is the importance of the ending of *An Inspector Calls*? Write about:
- how the ending of the play presents some important ideas
- how Priestley presents these ideas by the ways he writes.

Checklist for success

✔ Explain the effect of the ending and what we learn from it.

✔ Explain what you think Priestley wanted the ending to demonstrate to his audience.

✔ Use quotations to support your points.

✔ Explore the effects of language.

✔ Comment on the contexts of 1912 and 1944 where relevant.

End of chapter task

1 How does Priestley explore the idea of responsibility through the character Eric in *An Inspector Calls*? Write about:

- how Priestley presents Eric
- how Priestley uses Eric to explore ideas about responsibility.

Check your progress

- I can write clearly about ideas in the play.
- I can clearly explain how Priestley's methods explore ideas.
- I can show clear understanding of the contextual factors that influence audience interpretation.

- I can write critically about ideas in the play.
- I can analyse the ways Priestley's methods explore ideas.
- I can show thoughtful consideration of the contextual factors that influence audience interpretation.

The whole text:
Exploring themes

English Literature

You will read:
- extracts from across *An Inspector Calls*.

You will explore:
- the differences between the generations in *An Inspector Calls*
- ideas about social responsibility in the play
- how Priestley develops the theme of class.

English Language

You will read:
- an extract from an early-20th-century novel that highlights the difference between social classes.

You will explore:
- how to plan and respond to a critical evaluation question.

The contrast between the generations

Assessment objectives
• AO1, AO2, AO3

....

What ideas did Priestley want to convey to the different generations of 1944?

Priestley uses **characterisation** to create a representation of both the older and younger generation in *An Inspector Calls*.

Key term
....

characterisation: the creation of a fictional character

The older generation

In *An Inspector Calls,* Priestley presents Mr and Mrs Birling – representing the older generation – as sharing a similar view of the world.

1 Under each of the headings below, list everything you can remember about the older generation.

   a Actions   **b** Views   **c** Feelings

2 Using your lists, discuss in pairs what Priestley may have wanted the audience to think about the older generation and why.

The younger generation

The younger generation is represented by Sheila and Eric. Here, too, Priestley shows them as sharing a similar view of the world.

3 List what you can remember about the younger generation under the same three headings that were used in Task 1.

4 Discuss in pairs what Priestley may have wanted the audience to think about the younger generation and why.

5 Looking at your lists for each generation, where do you think Gerald fits in, in terms of actions, views and feelings? Why do you think this is?

6 Look at the language of the quotations below and write a short analysis of how each one patronises the younger generation or treats them like children.

- 'Now stop it, you two.'
- 'It's a lovely ring. Be careful with it.'
- 'You youngsters just remember what I said.'
- 'Why the devil do you want to go upsetting the child like that?'
- 'But I see no point in mentioning the subject – especially – (*indicating Sheila*)'
- 'They're overtired.'

7 In addition to this, the older generation are referred to formally, rather than by their first names. Write a short paragraph explaining the effect this has.

Priestley presents the circumstances and the beliefs of the older generation as very different from those of the younger generation.

8 For each of the scales below, decide where you would place the older generation and then the younger generation.

repentant	unrepentant
accepting of responsibility	not accepting of responsibility
socialist	capitalist
able to change	not able to change
likeable	unlikeable
friendly	unfriendly
confident	unconfident
powerful	weak

9 From the positions you allocated, note down what you consider to be the most significant differences between the generations.

When Mrs Birling comments on the effect Inspector Goole has had on Sheila, the Inspector replies: 'We often do on the young ones. They're more impressionable.'

10 Write a short explanation of why the younger generation are more impressionable and why it is more difficult for the older generation to change their ideas.

The generations and the context

Priestley wrote the play towards the end of the Second World War. He had fought in the First World War himself as a young man. We know that Priestley felt guilty about how many young men died following orders issued by middle-aged officers in the First World War.

11 What point might Priestley have been making about the generations and war? In what way does this link to the quote from Inspector Goole below?

'We are responsible for each other. And I tell you that the time will soon come when, if men will not learn that lesson, then they will be taught it in fire and blood and anguish.'

Checklist for success
· ·
- ✔ Briefly note three or four points that answer the question.
- ✔ Collect short quotations to support your points.
- ✔ Select language or devices that you will use to comment on effect.
- ✔ Note down any links to context.

Final task

12 Plan a response to the following question:

How does Priestley present some of the differences between the older and younger generations in *An Inspector Calls*? Write about:
- how the different generations respond to events and to each other
- how Priestley presents the different generations in the play.

The theme of responsibility

Assessment objectives
• AO1, AO2, AO3

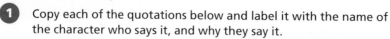

> **What ideas did Priestley want to convey to his audience about social responsibility?**

The theme of social responsibility in *An Inspector Calls*

One way that writers develop themes and ideas throughout a piece of writing is by revisiting the same topic or emotion in order to highlight the idea for the reader or audience.

In *An Inspector Calls*, Priestley presents a range of different views about personal responsibility.

1 Copy each of the quotations below and label it with the name of the character who says it, and why they say it.

a	'I can't accept any responsibility.'
b	'If we were all responsible for everything that happened to everybody we'd had anything to do with, it would be very awkward, wouldn't it?'
c	'So I'm really responsible?'
d	'I consider I did my duty.'
e	'We don't live alone. We are members of one body. We are responsible for each other.'
f	'There's every excuse for what both your mother and I did'
g	'The point is, you don't seem to have learnt anything.'
h	'a man has to mind his own business and look after himself and his own'
i	'It's my duty to keep labour costs down.'
j	'It's about time you learnt to face a few responsibilities.'
k	'But the way some of these cranks talk and write now, you'd think everybody has to look after everybody else, as if we were all mixed up together like bees in a hive.'

To whom is Gerald socially responsible?

Gerald had a six-month relationship with Daisy Renton. He knew what had happened to her and felt 'sorry' for her. However, in Act One he still believes that Birling did the right thing in sacking Eva Smith.

 Write a paragraph explaining why you think Gerald is not moved to take the side of the workers after hearing Daisy Renton's story.

Mr Birling's motivations for social responsibility

Despite offering 'thousands' to make amends for his actions, Mr Birling's feelings change when he starts to suspect that Inspector Goole's investigation was a hoax. He moves from being 'terrified' and offering 'thousands' to prevent a 'public scandal', to being 'amused'.

 What does this tell the audience about Mr Birling's motivations for socially responsible behaviour?

Social responsibility in the 1940s

It is important to remember that Priestley wrote *An Inspector Calls* in 1944, before the end of the Second World War. There was a Conservative government and the welfare state had not yet been implemented, but support for socialism in Britain was growing (see Chapter 1).

 Using what you know about the context of 1944, write a list of the key ideas you think Priestley wanted to convey about social responsibility.

Final task

 Plan an essay response to the following question:

What ideas did Priestley want to suggest to a contemporary audience about social responsibility?

Checklist for success

✔ Briefly note down three or four points that answer the question.

✔ Collect short quotations to support your points.

✔ Select language or devices that you will use to comment on effect.

✔ Note down any links to context.

The theme of social class

Assessment objectives
• AO1, AO2, AO3

What ideas did Priestley want to convey about class division?

The introduction of class

The theme of class is introduced at the very start of the play, where the stage directions describe the Birling's home:

> *The dining room of a large suburban house, belonging to a prosperous manufacturer.*

This stage direction contains clues to the class of the owners of this property. Remember that true aristocracy did not 'work' – they lived on income from land and the rents paid to them by tenants. However, in Victorian times industry and cities began to grow, and this led to some members of the middle class growing very wealthy, and able to invest in land and further business. By 1912, when the play is set, this had created a new social class with considerable power.

1 What social class does Mr Birling belong to? How does the stage direction show this?

Social mobility

The issue of social mobility (movement between the classes) is introduced when Priestley tells us that Mrs Birling is her husband's 'social superior'.

> Mrs Birling: *(reproachfully)* Arthur, you're not supposed to say such things –
> Mr Birling: Oh – come, come – I'm treating Gerald like one of the family.

2 What does this interaction between Mr and Mrs Birling indicate about their views on social conventions?

Sheila and Gerald's forthcoming marriage is another example of social mobility in practice – Gerald's family are upper class.

3 What hints does Priestley give in Act One that this marriage may not be to everyone's taste? List any evidence you can find.

The family has the trappings of upper-class life, but they are not quite comfortable in this role, especially in Gerald's presence. It seems as though Birling is mimicking the upper class – for example, Mr Birling says: 'Finchley told me it's exactly the same port your father gets from him'.

4 In pairs, discuss what this quotation reveals about Mr Birling's views on social mobility between the middle and upper classes.

5 Now consider Mr Birling's views about the working class. Discuss whether you think he would have the same views about movement between the lower and middle classes (see Lesson 4.3).

Perceptions of the lower class

When Gerald and Mrs Birling discuss Eva, they make several comments about the working class:

> 'Not if it was just after the holidays. They'd be all broke – if I know them.'
> 'As if a girl of that sort would ever refuse money!'

6 Copy the quotations and underline the key language choices in them. Label the parts of speech (use a dictionary if you need to) and add any connotations. Consider:

- the presumptions the characters make
- their tone
- the way they group all of the working class together.

Mr Birling makes presumptions about how working-class people behave:

'Have you any idea what happened to her after that? Get into trouble? Go on the streets?'

7 List all the presumptions that Mr Birling makes here. Add to the list by noting presumptions that other characters make about the working class during the play.

To juxtapose with the negative presumptions made about the working class by other characters, Priestley draws Eva Smith as a sympathetic character, with many positive attributes.

8 Copy and complete the table below to consider Eva's Smith's attributes and their effect on the audience.

Eva's positive attributes	Quotation	Effect on the audience
She's a good worker.		
She stands up for herself and others.		
She thinks stealing is wrong.		
She doesn't blame others for her misfortunes.		
She tries to protect the people in her life.		

9 Discuss with a partner which class of person you feel most sympathetic towards at the end of the play. Why do you think Priestley manipulated the audience's sympathies in this way?

Final task

10 Write a plan for the following essay question.

How does Priestley explore class in *An Inspector Calls*? Write about:

- the ideas about class in *An Inspector Calls*
- how Priestley presents these ideas by the way he writes.

Paper 1 Question 4: Critical evaluation

Assessment objective
• AO4

> ## How do I make my writing critical and evaluative?

What is a critical evaluation?

When you critically evaluate a text, you analyse it by identifying and interpreting themes and ideas, and by explaining how the writer's methods contribute to the effectiveness and impact of these ideas. To do this well, you need to use the same skills you put to work in Questions 2 and 3 of Paper 1:

- evaluating the effect of the language
- analysing the methods used by the writer and their impact
- selecting a range of relevant textual detail
- responding critically to the focus statement in the question.

The question will include a statement and you will have to explore the extent to which you agree or disagree with the statement. Often, there will be two parts to the statement. If this is the case, you should explore both.

 Read the question below and identify the key points in the statement that you need to write about.

Focus this part of your answer on line 4 ('but in revolt') until the end.

Having read this section of the text, one student said: 'This part of the text, where the women speak to each other, shows how horrible Mrs Shale and Miss Shale are. It makes me feel sorry for May.'

To what extent do you agree?

In your response, you could:

- write about your own impressions of Mrs and Miss Shale
- evaluate whether the writer makes you feel sorry for May
- support your opinions with references to the text.

Planning a critical evaluation

After you have read the question carefully, the first thing you should do is read the text and note down any parts that make you agree or disagree with the statement.

 Read the extract and note down any points that make you agree or disagree with the statement.

In the extract, May, a lower-class girl, visits the aristocratic Mrs Shale and her daughter Miss Shale to ask them to reconsider their decision to throw her family out of their home. Earlier in the text, May refused to open a door for Miss Shale and this is why May's family are being evicted.

At something past eleven o'clock, a footman approached her, and said curtly, 'You are to go up to my lady; follow me.' May followed, shaking with weakness and apprehension, burning at the same time with pride all but in revolt. Conscious of nothing on the way, she found herself in a large room, where sat the two ladies, who for some moments spoke together about a topic of the day placidly. Then the elder seemed to become aware of the girl who stood before her.

'You are the Rocketts' elder daughter?'

Oh, the metallic voice of Lady Shale! How gratified she would have been could she have known how it bruised the girl's pride!

'Yes, my lady—'

'And why do you want to see me?'

'I wish to apologise – most sincerely – to your ladyship – for my behaviour of last evening—'

'Oh, indeed!' the listener interrupted contemptuously. 'I am glad you have come to your senses. But your apology must be offered to Miss Shale – if my daughter cares to listen to it.'

May had foreseen this. It was the critical evauation bitterest moment of her ordeal. Flushing scarlet, she turned towards the younger woman.

'Miss Shale, I beg your pardon for what I said yesterday – I beg you to forgive my rudeness – my impertinence—'

Her voice would go no further; there came a choking sound. Miss Shale allowed her eyes to rest triumphantly for an instant on the troubled face and figure, then remarked to her mother –

'It's really nothing to me, as I told you. I suppose this person will leave the room now?'

It was fated that May Rockett should go through with her purpose and gain her end. But fate alone (which meant in this case the subtlest preponderance of one impulse over another) checked her on the point of a burst of passion which would have startled Lady Shale and Miss Hilda out of their cold-blooded complacency. In the silence May's blood gurgled at her ears, and she tottered with dizziness.

'You may go,' said Lady Shale.

From 'A Daughter of the Lodge' by George Gissing, 1901

Once you have read the text and made notes, you should select four key points that respond to the statement. They can agree or disagree with the statement, or they can be a mixture of both. These will form your topic sentences at the start of each paragraph.

3 Bullet-point your four key responses to the statement. For each one, select quotations to support your statements. You can use just one quotation for each point but it is better to use a range.

You also need to consider the writer's methods and their effects. It is useful to link the effects to the focus statement in the question.

4 Annotate your selected quotations with the writer's methods. Consider individual word choices and any language devices.

5 Then annotate your language selections with their connotations and effects – what they make the reader think, feel and imagine.

Introduction to a critical evaluation

Your four-point plan will form the main part of your essay. However, you should also write a short introduction, in which you answer the question, explaining the extent to which you agree with the statement and why.

You could begin your introduction in one of the following ways:

- I fully agree with … because

- I partly agree with … because

- I agree to some extent that … because

- I disagree somewhat with … because

- I both agree and disagree with … because

6 Write your introduction. If there are two parts to the statement, remember to agree or disagree with *both* parts.

Literature link

This text shows the kind of restrictions that were placed on members of the lower classes and the humiliation they could be subjected to if they tried to overcome them. May's situation echoes Eva's uncomfortable conversations with both Mr and Mrs Birling when she tries to speak up for herself. It reminds us how impossible it would have been for Eva to have a public relationship with Gerald or Eric.

Writing your critical evaluation

You are now ready to write your full response. Remember – it is the *quality* of your explanation that will gain you the most credit, not the naming of techniques alone.

A complete paragraph should:

- state if your point makes you agree or disagree with the statement
- explain your interpretation and why you agree or disagree
- give the quotation that supports your point
- identify the methods(s) being used and how they create your view – for example, via their literal meaning/the picture they create/the senses they stimulate/the connotations they evoke.

Look at the following paragraph. The highlighting shows which part of the mark scheme is being met.

> *I fully agree that the writer presents Mrs Shale as horrible as the writer creates the impression that she is a cold and unpleasant woman, not just in what she says to May, which is patronising and superior, but also in the way she says it. By using the phrase 'metallic voice', the writer helps the reader to imagine the unfriendly tone of her words, which would be grating and high pitched and without variation. This suggests a lack of feeling and empathy for May. The adjective 'metallic' also has connotations of strength and hardness, which makes us feel that Lady Shale lacks self-doubt and compassion. This is why she is so horrible and why the reader begins to pity May.*

evaluating the effect of the language on the writer
analysing the methods used by the writer and their impact
selecting a range of relevant textual detail
responding critically to the focus statement

Final task

 Using the modelled paragraph to help you, write your answer from your plan. Allow yourself approximately 20 minutes.

End of chapter task

1 Look at each of the essay plans you have completed for this chapter. Select one of them and turn it into a full essay response. You should not have the text with you when you write the response. Time yourself: spend no more than 40 minutes on this task.

Check your progress

- I can write clearly about themes in the play.
- I can clearly explain how Priestley's methods explore themes.
- I can show clear understanding of the contextual factors that influenced Priestley's writing.

- I can write critically about themes in the play.
- I can analyse the ways Priestley's methods explore themes.
- I can show thoughtful consideration of the contextual factors that influenced Priestley's writing.

The whole text: Exploring character

English Literature

You will read:

- sections from across *An Inspector Calls*.

You will explore:

- your understanding of Mr and Mrs Birling and their role in the play
- your understanding of Sheila's and Gerald's roles in the play
- the purpose of the character Inspector Goole.

English Language

You will read:

- a description of a character.

You will explore:

- how to show, not tell, in your narrative writing
- how to craft language.

Mr and Mrs Birling and their role in the play

Assessment objectives
• AO1, AO2, AO3

. . . .

What do Mr and Mrs Birling represent in *An Inspector Calls?*

Drawing together ideas from across the play

Now you have read the whole play, you need to draw together what you have learned about each character. This allows you to see whether they have changed or developed in the course of the action, and to consider how Priestley has used the characters to symbolise particular themes or ideas.

Identifying Mr Birling's key moments

To gain an overview of a character, you need to track what they say and do across each act and sometimes a part of each act. It can help to organise your tracking so that you can see patterns clearly.

 Copy the table below onto a piece of A3 paper. Work through the six sections of the play, using your notes from Chapters 3 and 4 – where you investigated the character of Mr Birling in depth – to complete columns A–D. Complete columns E and F with your own ideas and observations.

	A	B	C	D	E	F
	Act One (until Inspector Goole's entrance)	Act One (until Sheila sees the photo)	Act Two (Birling's entrance until Gerald's exit)	Act Two (Gerald's exit until end)	Act Three (until Gerald's return)	Act Three (until the end)
Character	In control, confident. Likes to be in charge: 'Are you listening, Sheila? This concerns you too.'					
Contribution to themes	Holds capitalist values: 'a man has to mind his own business and look after himself and his own'. Is concerned about class: 'She comes from an old country family – landed people and so forth – so it's only natural.'					

How audience is intended to feel	Dislike his beliefs: 'Except of course in Russia, which will always be behindhand naturally'. Think he is ignorant: 'unsinkable, absolutely unsinkable'.					
Language use and devices from the quotations selected	Aphorism: 'a man has to mind his own business and look after himself and his own.' Arrogant adverbs: 'naturally', 'absolutely'. Dramatic irony: 'unsinkable'					

Identifying Mrs Birling's key moments

Mrs Birling features in the play less than Mr Birling, but her contribution is still significant.

2 Copy the table below and complete it to track the character of Mrs Birling throughout the play. Use your notes from Chapter 6 to complete columns A–C. Use your own ideas and observations to complete columns D and E.

	A	B	C	D	E
	Act One (until her exit)	Act Two (during Gerald's story)	Act Two (until the end of the act)	Act Three (until Gerald's return)	Act Three (until the end)
Character	She isn't a likeable character: 'rather cold woman'. In charge of her adult children: 'What an expression, Sheila!'				

	A	B	C	D	E
Contribution to themes	She accepts the role of women: 'You'll have to get used to that, just as I had.' She believes it is important to keep up higher-class appearances: '(reproachfully) Arthur, you're not supposed to say such things.'				
Way audience is intended to feel	Wary, as she has a quiet control of the room, although she does not say much: '(rising. The others rise) Yes, of course, dear. Well – don't keep Gerald in here too long. Eric – I want you a minute.'				
Language use and devices from the quotations selected	Adjectives: 'cold' Adverbs: 'reproachfully' Imperatives: 'don't keep Gerald in here too long.'				

Character development through the play

The information you have collected in the table can help you see how those two characters develop throughout the play, and if and how they change.

 3 Use the tables you created, and your knowledge of the play as a whole, to support you in answering the following questions. Write your answers in full sentences and make sure you provide quotations as evidence.

   a Do the Birlings stay the same throughout the play or do their personalities change? If they do change, what triggers this?

   b What are the Birlings' attitudes towards social class/position?

   c Do you think either of the Birlings' attitudes towards women develops or changes through the play? If so, how and why?

   d Do you think that the Birlings' attitude towards responsibility develops or changes through the play?

   e Which of the two characters do you find more sympathetic? Give reasons for your answer.

4 Considering the themes that Priestley explores through Mr and Mrs Birling, what do you think these characters represent? Create a bullet-point list for each character.

Language focus

When writing your essay response in the exam, you will need to make AO2 language comments about the effect of Priestley's language choices, as well as making AO1 comments to show your understanding of characters and themes.

5 Look at the language choices you selected in your tables. For each one, create a 'connotation-and-effect' spider diagram. Mr Birling's spider diagram has been started for you.

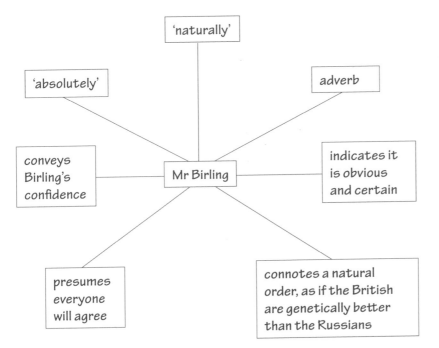

Final task

6 Write a response to the following question, focusing on the character of *either* Mr Birling *or* Mrs Birling.

How does Priestley explore the idea of responsibility through either Mr Birling or Mrs Birling? Write about:

- the ideas about responsibility in *An Inspector Calls*
- how Priestley presents the idea of responsibility through either Mr Birling or Mrs Birling.

Sheila's and Gerald's roles in the play

Assessment objectives
- AO1, AO2, AO3

How are Sheila and Gerald presented in *An Inspector Calls*?

Sheila's journey

Arguably, Sheila is the character who changes most through the course of the play. Considering her character both before and after the pivotal moment – when she realises her role in Eva's death – will help you identify these changes.

1 Copy the two outlines of Sheila below and label one 'Before' and the other 'After'. Track through the play and add notes on Sheila's behaviour, thoughts and feelings around the outside of your outlines, before and after her pivotal moment.

- Try to write your comments in pairs, to show the differences between before and after.
- Include a quotation for each point that you make inside your outline.

For example:

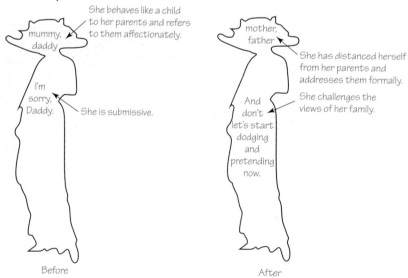

She behaves like a child to her parents and refers to them affectionately.

mummy, daddy

I'm sorry, Daddy.

She is submissive.

Before

mother, father

She has distanced herself from her parents and addresses them formally.

And don't let's start dodging and pretending now.

She challenges the views of her family.

After

Gerald's journey

Gerald is an interesting character to track, because in Act Two he seems to have changed, but by the end of the play we realise that perhaps he has not learned his lesson in the way that Sheila has.

2 Draw three male outlines, one to represent Gerald in each act of the play. Track through the play and add notes to the outside of your outline that show Gerald's behaviour, thoughts or feelings in each act. Inside each outline, include a quotation for each point that you make.

Thinking about character

Your character outlines will not only help you think about the characters, they will also aid your understanding of the themes which Priestley explores through the characters.

3 Add points and quotations to your character outlines that show Sheila and Gerald's thoughts and feelings about each of the following themes:

- responsibility
- class
- the role of women
- workers' rights.

4 Look back at your character outlines and answer the following question. Write in full sentences and make sure you provide quotations as evidence.

Which character do you think changes more in the play, Sheila or Gerald? Consider:

- the changes in each character's behaviour
- the changes in their feelings towards other characters
- the changes in their thoughts about the themes explored in the play.

Language focus

You have collected a series of quotations to support your points about character, but it is important that the quotations you have chosen also include interesting and effective language so that you can make detailed AO2 comments about them.

5 **a** Look back at the quotations you have written in your character outlines and underline the key language choices that you would be able to analyse.

b For each underlined word or device, write an analysis of the effect of Priestley's language choice.

c Select one language choice for Sheila and one for Gerald. Explain why you think Priestley used the language he did.

Final task

6 Write a response to the following question, focusing on the character of *either* Sheila *or* Gerald.

How does Priestley present change in either Sheila or Gerald in *An Inspector Calls*?

Write about:

- the ideas about how Sheila or Gerald changes in *An Inspector Calls*
- how Priestley presents Sheila or Gerald as changing by the ways he writes.

Evaluating the role of the Inspector

Assessment objectives
• AO1, AO2

What is the significance of the Inspector?

When writing about characters, it is useful to have a clear **premise** on which to base your arguments and comments. Outline your premise in your introduction, then explore and build upon it in the rest of your essay.

How Priestley establishes Inspector Goole

In Chapter 7, you considered the role of Inspector Goole and what he represents. You might have decided that he is symbolic of socialism or that he is a mouthpiece for Priestley's views. This would be your premise.

1 Write a brief explanation of what you think the character of Inspector Goole represents and why.

Priestley immediately establishes Inspector Goole as an influential and powerful character, despite the fact that he appears to be lower middle class, rather than upper middle class, like the Birlings.

2 Look at the interaction between the two men below and discuss with a partner how Priestley shows the Inspector taking control.

BIRLING:	Have a glass of port – or a little whisky?
INSPECTOR:	No, thank you, Mr Birling. I'm on duty.
[...]	
BIRLING:	I was alderman for years – and Lord Mayor two years ago – and I'm still on the Bench – so I know the Brumley police officers pretty well – and I thought I'd never seen you before.
INSPECTOR:	Quite so.
BIRLING:	Well, what can I do for you? Some trouble about a warrant?
INSPECTOR:	No, Mr Birling.
BIRLING:	*(after a pause, with a touch of impatience)* Well, what is it then?

3 Look at the language in this interaction. Note down the purpose and the effect of each of the following features:

a Birling's initial imperative

b the pauses in Birling's list

c Inspector Goole's **laconicism**

d Birling's use of interrogatives.

Key term

laconicism: the practice of saying very few words

4 Discuss with a partner whether these interpretations support your premise. If they do not, reconsider your premise.

Inspector Goole as supernatural

Many people think Inspector Goole has an element of the supernatural about him.

5 Note down any evidence you can find for this. Try to find quotations to support your view. Consider the following:

- his name
- Sheila's response to him
- his power
- his message
- the play's ending.

Inspector Goole and responsibility

When Sheila wants to stay to listen to Gerald's role in Daisy Renton's life, Inspector Goole explains, 'we have to share something. If there's nothing else, we'll have to share our guilt.'

6 Discuss with a partner what this tells the audience about the role of Inspector Goole in relation to the theme of social responsibility.

Inspector Goole's final speech is a plea for the Birlings – and for Priestley's audience – to show social responsibility:

'We don't live alone. We are members of one body. We are responsible for each other.'

7 Annotate the effect of the quotation, considering:

- the **anaphora**
- the contrasting of 'alone' and 'members'
- the use of the abstract noun 'body'
- the personal pronoun 'we'
- the simple, **declarative** sentences.

8 Write a paragraph explaining how these language devices emphasise the importance of Inspector Goole's message.

Key term

anaphora: the repetition of a word or phrase at the beginning of sentences or clauses

declarative: a sentence form that gives information

Final task

9 Plan your response to the following exam question:

How does Priestley present the character of the Inspector in *An Inspector Calls?* Write about:

- how the Inspector responds to other characters
- how Priestley presents the Inspector by the way he writes.

Paper 1 Question 5: Narrative

Assessment objective
• AO5

How can I respond to a narrative writing question?

Narrative writing
In Paper 1 Question 5, you may be asked to write a story, or the opening of a story. When writing a short story, it is important to engage your readers by helping them to develop an emotional reaction to the character(s). This reaction can be positive or negative.

Developing character
In a narrative, usually in the opening exposition, the writer will introduce the main character. The purpose of this is to give background information about the character and to create an emotional response to them.

Read this description of a character.

> Norman, the assistant to the assistant manager, patrolled the corridor with clockwork regularity. It was very important to Norman that he exercised his duties with expert precision. Every thirty minutes, his grey-suited form, clipboard in tow, would circuit the office booths, diligently recording any slight misdemeanour or distractedness in the staff.

1 Make brief notes on your overall emotional response to the character.

2 Identity the key language in the description that helped develop your emotional response, and jot these down. Add annotations that indicate what these parts made you think, feel and imagine about the character.

Showing, not telling
The best writers subtly manipulate a response in the reader by showing them images designed to generate certain feelings, rather than by outlining a character's personality explicitly. For example, rather than stating that a character is mean, a writer might show meanness through the character's actions.

3 Write a list of things that you could include in the exposition about a character to indicate that they have a cold, without explicitly stating this fact. Consider the following:
- What would the character look like?
- What might they be doing?
- How might they sound?
- What taste might be in their mouth?
- How might they feel?

4 Work with a partner to create a list of things you might include in the exposition about a character who is grieving and who you wanted your reader to feel sorry for. Think about the different ways that grief might affect someone:

- What happens to their posture? Their voice? Their facial expression?
- What might their limbs feel like? Their heart?
- What do they do? How does crying begin, especially when they're trying not to?
- What does the rest of the world seem like to them?

5 Spend 10 minutes turning your notes into a short exposition paragraph of the character, like the one about the businessman Norman.

Crafting language

The words that writers choose in narratives have a significant impact on how their readers interpret characters. Even words that have similar meanings can have different implications and create very different feelings.

6 The verbs below all mean 'walk'. Rank them in order of how fast you consider them to be, from slowest to quickest:

- walk
- swagger
- strut
- tiptoe
- stroll
- traipse.

7 Look again at the list of verbs. This time, rank them in order of how confident you consider the walker to be.

8 Now look at these verbs, which are used in the description of Norman in Task 1. In pairs, discuss their effect:

a patrolled
b exercised
c circuit
d recording.

Noun phrases can also play a very important role in crafting a character. Look at the nouns and noun phrases used in the description of Norman.

- assistant to the assistant manager
- corridor
- clockwork regularity
- duties
- expert precision
- thirty minutes
- grey-suited form
- clipboard
- office booths
- staff.

9 What atmosphere do these nouns and noun phrases help to create?

> ### Checklist for success
> ✔ Show, don't tell.
> ✔ Carefully select your verbs.
> ✔ Carefully select your noun phrases.
> ✔ Aim to create an emotional response from the reader.

Final task

10 Write the opening part of a story about a character who is very emotional.

End of chapter task

1. Inspector Goole is a key character in the play. He drives all the action, as each character reveals their role in Eva Smith's life. Many of the themes are explored through his character, the most significant of which is the theme of social responsibility.

In Act One, the Inspector says, 'But after all it's better to ask for the earth than to take it.' Using this quote as a starting point, answer the question below:

How does Priestley explore the idea of our responsibility towards others in *An Inspector Calls*? Write about:

- the ideas about our responsibility towards others in *An Inspector Calls*
- how Priestley presents these ideas by the ways he writes.

Check your progress

- I can write clearly about characters and themes in the play.
- I can clearly explain how Priestley's methods explore themes through characters.
- I can show clear understanding of the contextual factors that influenced Priestley's writing.

- I can write critically about characters and themes in the play.
- I can analyse the ways Priestley's methods explore themes through characters.
- I can show thoughtful consideration of the contextual factors that influenced Priestley's writing.

Exam practice

English Literature

You will read:

- sections from across the whole of *An Inspector Calls.*

You will explore:

- how to plan your response to a character-based question in the exam
- how to plan your response to a theme-based question in the exam
- how to express your ideas clearly and coherently in an essay form
- how to evaluate the quality of essay responses.

Understanding a character-based question

Assessment objectives
- AO1, AO2, AO3, AO4

> **How should I respond to a character-based question in the exam?**

The Assessment objectives

The question on *An Inspector Calls* will test all four of the Assessment objectives:

- **AO1:** Show understanding of the text with a critical style, supported by references to the text and quotations.
- **AO2:** Analyse language, form and structure with accurate subject terminology.
- **AO3:** Show understanding of the relationship between texts and the contexts in which they were written.
- **AO4:** Use a range of vocabulary, sentences, punctuation and spelling for clarity and effect.

1 Look at each of the skills below and decide if they are AO1, AO2, AO3 or AO4:

  a referring to Priestley's life

  b using quotations

  c commenting on how the 1944 audience would have responded

  d analysing the effect of language

  e using subject terminology

  f using a range of sentence structures

  g exploring the meaning of themes

  h referring to events in the play

  i using accurate spelling and punctuation

  j analysing the effect of structure

  k explaining the context of 1912 or 1944.

The character-based question

In the exam, you will have a choice of two questions. One of these may be a character-based question. This will ask you to focus on the role of a particular character. It may also ask you to focus on a particular thing about that character, such as how much they change or part of their personality.

2 Read the exam-style questions. Note down what each one is asking you to focus on.

01 How far does Priestley present Gerald as untrustworthy in
An Inspector Calls?
Write about:
- what Gerald says and does that is untrustworthy
- how Priestley's writing presents Gerald as untrustworthy.

02 How far does Priestley present Mrs Birling as an unsympathetic
character? Write about:
- what Mrs Birling says and does in the play
- how Priestley presents her in the ways he writes.

Your premise

Once you understand the question, you need to decide on your response
and your premise about the purpose of the character. This premise
should introduce an idea about what you think the character represents.
You should then argue this interpretation throughout your essay.

3 Think about the second exam-style question in Task 2 above and
note down what your premise would be. Consider:
- Mrs Birling's views and behaviour in the play
- what Mrs Birling might represent
- Priestley's political views
- how the audience feels about Mrs Birling at the end of the play.

Planning a response to a character-based question

Next, you need to plan. The format below is useful for a character question:

1   Introduction: answer the question and explain your premise
2   How the character is established
3   How the character begins to develop
4   How the character continues to develop
5   How the character ends the play
6   Conclusion: how context or other factors support your premise.

Remember, in a good response, each of your paragraphs should support
and build on your premise. To do this, you should include the following
in each paragraph:
- a key argument to support your premise (AO1)
- quotations from the text as evidence of your argument (AO1)
- an exploration of the effects of the language Priestley uses (AO2)
- consideration of how context influences your interpretation (AO3).

4 Choose one of the exam-style questions in Task 2 and write
your six-paragraph plan for it, including topic sentences, key
quotations, effective language features and key contexts.

Developing your response

Assessment objectives
• AO1, AO2, AO3

How can I do justice to my ideas through the way I write?

Your introduction

Your introduction should be a brief but direct answer to the question. Higher-level responses will introduce a premise that makes clear what line of argument you will follow in the rest of the essay. The example below is a response to the question about Mrs Birling in Lesson 10.1.

> Mrs Birling is presented as the archetypal upper-class woman of her time and, as a result of her upholding the manners, traditions and values of the upper classes, her character is very unsympathetic. Priestley uses her character to symbolise the negativity of the upper classes and their lack of social responsibility. Making her unsympathetic is key to the way Priestley manipulates the audience to agree with his socialist views. Mrs Birling looks down on and expects subservience from anyone lower down the social hierarchy, and she speaks with a consistently superior tone of voice – despite her actions toward Eva being far from superior. Priestley also uses Mrs Birling to criticise the inconsistent and unreliable use of charity to support the working class in 1912 – such as the Brumley Women's Charity Organisation that turned Eva away due to personal prejudice. This allows Priestley to illustrate to the audience how necessary the development of a more reliable and equitable welfare state was in 1944.

 1   In the student's paragraph above, identify the following.

   a   a clear statement that answers the question

   b   a clear premise about the purpose of Mrs Birling's character

   c   a clear explanation of the methods Priestley uses to achieve his purpose

   d   a second premise about the purpose of Mrs Birling's character

   e   a link to context.

Writing effective paragraphs

Ideally, each ensuing paragraph should include the following (though not necessarily in this order):

   •   a relevant point about how Priestley presents Mrs Birling (as unsympathetic or not)

   •   support for the point with reference to the text – preferably an embedded quotation

   •   an explanation of the methods Priestley has used in the quotation (e.g. stage directions, tone of voice)

- a zoom into Priestley's language choices and their effects
- a link between the points you have made in the paragraph and your original premise
- a reference to context (where relevant).

2 Identify each of the features listed above, in the following example paragraph.

Priestley makes it very clear that Mrs Birling is an unsympathetic character when he describes her as a 'rather cold woman'. By using stage directions, Priestley makes this feature fixed, suggesting that it will have a significant role in the play as it unfolds. The adjective 'cold' creates the image of an unfeeling character who is not kind and loving but harsh and detached. It indicates that she lacks empathy and this presentation through the actor would immediately make the audience dislike her. Priestley establishes Mrs Birling as an unlikeable character from the very beginning so that the audience will begin to judge her superiority and belief that her class is better, despite it lacking the empathy necessary for social responsibility.

Thinking about AO4

You can improve your AO4 mark by thinking carefully about how to link your ideas throughout your writing. There are several ways to do this:

- Refer to the play's chronology – whether the event happens before or after something else.
- Use a conjunctive adverbial to develop a point.
- Refer to your premise and how it is further proved by each successive point.

3 Look at your essay plan and note down how you will link each idea.

The vocabulary choices that you make will also affect your AO4 mark.

4 a For each character, bullet-point a list of up to five adjectives that describe their personality or behaviour.

b Use a thesaurus to find more nuanced words that mean similar things. Write down any alternatives that match your thoughts about the characters.

5 Now write your response in full paragraphs to the exam-style question, based on the plan you created in Lesson 10.1.

Peer- and self-assessment

Assessment objectives
- AO1, AO2, AO3

- -

What level am I working at?

Understanding the mark scheme

There are 12 marks available for AO1 and 12 marks available for AO2. There are only 6 marks available for AO3. This means that, proportionately, your essay should be split roughly like this:

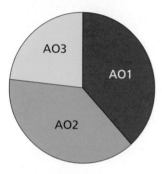

The mark scheme for the *An Inspector Calls* question is numbered 1–6, with 6 the highest mark.

What are the features of a clear and well-explained response?

A level 4 response needs to be clear and well explained.

AO1	• At this level, you will show you have **understood the task clearly**, so your points will be **relevant**. You will comment on **both the passage and the wider play**.
	• You will make **clear and suitable references** to the text (they will support your points effectively) and your **use of quotations should be clearly explained**. It is likely you have embedded most or all of them in your writing.
AO2	• You will **explain the writer's methods** clearly so that the marker knows what particular things the author has done.
	• You will explain clearly what the effects of the writer's choices are.
	• You will use some **useful subject terminology** (for example, reference to 'adjectives' or 'irony') in a correct way, supporting the points you make.
AO3	• You show clear understanding of how some ideas about context link to the set task.
	• You do not 'bolt on' irrelevant references about social or historical ideas, or about the writer's views, but **show a straightforward** link to the task.

What are the features of a convincing, analytical response?

A level 6 response needs to be clear and well explained, but also convincing and analytical.

AO1	• At this level, you have a **complete, deep understanding of the task** and are able to put forward a **sustained response**. This is why your premise is important. You take in the bigger picture and are able to connect your ideas into a coherent overall view of the task and text.
	• Any references you make to the text are **extremely carefully selected** and are more fruitful than alternatives you might have chosen.
	• You show exploration and more than one interpretation of a wide range of language, form and structural aspects.
AO2	• You **analyse the writer's methods**, drilling down into detail where needed, or expanding interpretations to make **interesting and useful links**.
	• You use a wide range of subject terminology, and can explore in detail the potential and varying effects on the reader.
AO3	• Your comments on context are convincing and significantly add to your analysis of the text.
	• You reveal **rich insights** into the writer's motives and the overall 'message' of the text, all linked convincingly to the task set.

1. Read your response to the exam question on page 123. Add your own annotations to it, linking your comments to the Assessment objectives. Look at the way it has been done to the example student paragraph below.

AO1: shows a clear understanding of the text and character

AO2: subject terminology

Mrs Birling's superior attitude and lack of empathy with the lower classes furthers Priestley's depiction of her as an unsympathetic character. As Sheila identifies, she builds a 'wall' between herself and Eva Smith, simply because she is of a different class, because in 1912 the classes were much more separate. When questioned about Eva, she says, 'though naturally I don't know anything about this girl'. The adverb 'naturally' indicates that it is clear and obvious that she won't know Eva because she is so far above her in the hierarchy. It also connotes a natural order as if it is their nature, rather than their money that separates them.

AO1: relevant textual detail

AO3: relevant link to context

AO1: relevant quotation

AO2: examination of writer's methods

(2) Read the following essay response to the exam-style question on page 123 and the examiner's comments.

Student A

In 'An Inspector Call's, Priestley presents Mrs Birling as an unsympathetic character because she is unsympathetic to others and the audience do not like her. She is used by Priestley to show that upper-class snobbery is horrible.

> AO1 – short explanation of character

In the opening of the play, Priestley establishes her as bossy and abrupt to her family: 'Now stop it, you two'. This shows that she feels that she can order her children around and that they should do what she says, even though they are both young adults and Sheila is going to be married. She even bosses her husband around, although he is male, perhaps because she is higher in the social hierarchy than him, which was more important and fixed in 1912.

> AO1 – clear understanding of character with supporting reference

> AO3 – some implicit and explicit understanding of context

When it comes to Eva Smith, Mrs Birling is a very unsympathetic character as she is so snobby about her that does not seem to care that she has died. She says, 'I don't suppose for a moment that we can understand why the girl committed suicide. Girls of that class –' which shows she believes that Eva could never be understood by her because she is so different, simply because she is lower class. The plural 'girls' groups all working class young women together, as if they all behave in exactly the same way because of their class. 'Girls' is also patronising and shows a lack of respect for these young female workers. This makes Mrs Birling very unsympathetic as her snobbery makes her seem ignorant because she assumes the worst of Eva simply because she is lower class when, in actual fact, Eva behaves morally throughout and it is Mrs Birling's family who behave badly.

> AO1 – clear understanding of character and text with supporting reference

> AO2 – clear comment on the effect of writer's methods (language)

> AO1 – clear response to the task and text

AO1 – clear understanding of character and text with supporting reference

AO2 – clear comment on the effect of writer's methods (language)

At the end of the play, Mrs. Birling does not seem to have changed at all and has not learned anything from the Inspector. When Sheila says she is behaving exactly how she was before, Mrs Birling says, 'Well, why shouldn't we?' Her question shows a complete lack of understanding of Sheila's feelings and the message of the Inspector. It also indicates that she is arrogant because the question indicates she doesn't even feel challenged by what has happened. In fact, she is 'amused', which indicates she finds it funny and something to be laughed about – this is simply because she doesn't care about working class people like Eva and their story and that is why she is such an unsympathetic character.

AO2 – clear comment on the effect of writer's methods (language)

AO1 – explained response to the task and text

Examiner's comment

This response shows a clear AO1 understanding of the text and character. AO1 quotations and textual references are relevant and AO2 comments on writer's methods are clear. More exploration of AO3 contextual links would have added greater depth and insight.

3 Evaluate this answer against the level 4 and level 6 marking criteria on pages 126–7 and decide which level you think the response is closest to.

4 Next, read Student B's response and the examiner's annotations and decide whether it is better or worse than Student A's. Note down what level you think it is.

Student B

Throughout 'An Inspector Calls', Priestley presents Mrs Birling as an unsympathetic character, depicting her as a 'rather cold woman' whose interactions with every other character, including her own husband, appear both critical and lacking in empathy. She is presented as an archetypal villain with Priestley using her as a caricature of the selfishness and negativity of the upper classes and their views of the lower classes in order to criticise the class divide still present in 1946.

AO1 – effective reference to support explanation

AO1 – a perceptive response to task and text

AO3 – implicit understanding of context

Mrs Birling's superior attitude is immediately established by Priestley through Mrs Birling's speech: '(reproachfully) Arthur, you're not supposed to say such things –' Her use of her husband's name adds a sincerity to her statement – she means it and wants him to listen. Clearly, these conventions matter to her and there is a little embarrassment that Gerald, her social superior, is witnessing her husband's lack of formality.

AO2 and AO1 – identification of writer's methods with supporting textual detail

AO1 – clear understanding of writer's methods

AO1 and AO3 – clear response to text with implicit consideration of context

After Priestley has established her in this way, it is hardly surprising to see her snobbery about Eva Smith's death. In fact, her response is almost callous, describing it as 'absurd business'. She gives no consideration to the life that has been lost or the causes of Eva's suicide. Instead, she focuses on class; Priestley's use of the adjective 'absurd' highlights how ridiculous the idea of a connection between a working class girl and her family is to her. The word has connotations of irrationality and the illogical, showing how she believes that 'naturally' the death of a lower class girl could have nothing to do with her family.

AO1 – development of response with integrated references to the text

AO2 – examination of the effect of writer's methods with accurate subject terminology

AO1 – precise and judicious references to the text

The metaphorical 'wall' of snobbery that Mrs Birling has built between her class and Eva's is further evidenced by the way she stereotypes them, presuming that a girl of 'that sort' would never refuse money. The noun 'sort' conveys Mrs Birling's judgement. She has already decided her views about Eva, not based on her actions or the facts, but on her class. She considers herself so separate from those 'girls' that the idea of Gerald having a relationship with one of them is 'disgusting' to her. The use of this present participle conveys the depth of Mrs Birling's feelings: her response to close contact with the working class is visceral. She finds it simply repulsive and sordid.

AO1 – precise and judicious references to the text

AO2 – developed analysis and interpretation of writer's methods with accurate subject terminology

This absolute snobbery certainly makes her unsympathetic to a modern audience, as the class divide has reduced significantly since 1912 and her assertions appear pretentious. Even to Priestley's 1946 audience, her view would have been considered by most as extreme, particularly given the way the classes had mixed – to positive rather than negative effect – during the Second World War.

AO3 – detailed link and thoughtful consideration of contextual factors

Overall, it is her snobbery and her superior attitude that make her such an unsympathetic character, particularly as she does not change. Unfortunately, the shock when she briefly looks 'terrified' does not last and by the end of the play she is 'smiling'. It seems that her inability to change despite all of the evidence presented to her to undo her prejudice is what truly makes her an unsympathetic character and in this way Priestley uses her to advocate exactly that: change.

AO1 – precise and judicious references to the text

AO1 – critical, conceptualised response to text and task

Examiner's comment

This is a convincingly argued AO1 response that confidently moves through the play, linking ideas and exploring them thoroughly. References to AO3 social context are used to support the overall argument, and AO2, Priestley's use of language, is explored in depth, with real evidence towards the end of the response of critical, conceptualised thinking.

5. Look at the response which you think was better. Make a list of the features or points that you feel make it better.

Theme and theme-through-character questions

Assessment objectives
- AO1, AO2, AO3

How should I respond to theme-based questions?

A theme-based question will identify a specific theme and ask you to write about how ideas linked to the theme are explored and developed.

The theme-based question

To start, carefully read the question and underline the focus, as you would for a character-based question.

 Look at the question below and identify its focus.

> **0 3** How does Priestley present the differences in age in *An Inspector Calls*?
>
> You should write about:
> - the ideas about age that are explored
> - how these ideas are developed in the play.

You may come across a theme-through-character question. In these questions, you must still write about the theme identified in the question, but you should look at the theme through the lens of the character named in the question.

Planning a theme or theme-through-character question

In order to write about a theme, consider where that theme is explored in the play. In your mind, run through the events of the play in order – this will ensure you do not miss anything out. You can then select from your list the ideas you think you could write about most effectively.

 List the occasions in the play when the theme of age is explored.

To write a response at the highest levels, your ideas need to be linked and developed. It may help you to consider one or two ideas that you want to explore in depth, then find examples from the text to support your thinking. For example:

> The characters from the younger generation have a great capacity for change and to create social change:
> - Inspector Goole tells Mrs Birling that he often makes an impression on the 'young ones'.

- Sheila, as part of the younger generation, changes a lot because of the Inspector and calls for social change, beginning with her parents' attitudes: '(*passionately*) You're pretending everything's just as it was before.'

Notice how the ideas in both the bullet points support the *overall* point about age – that the younger generation have the capacity for change and to create social change.

3 Using the information above, and your notes from Lessons 3.4 and 8.1 to help you, write down two ideas that you could write about regarding the theme of age, and two examples you could use to exemplify them.

4 Write a six-paragraph plan to respond to the question. Make sure you include quotations to support your argument.

Writing effective paragraphs

At a basic level, each paragraph about the passage should include:

- a relevant point about how Priestley presents the theme of age
- support for that point with direct reference to the text (preferably an embedded quotation)
- an explanation of the methods Priestley uses in the quotation (e.g. stage directions, tone)
- an explanation of any links to context/other themes/characters
- a zoom in on Priestley's language choices and their effects
- a link between the points you have made in the paragraph and your original premise
- a reference to context (where relevant).

5 Read the following exemplar paragraph and identify the features listed above.

Priestley makes it very clear that Eva is 'young'. The word is used almost every time that she is mentioned and her personal story unfolds. The adjective indicates a sense of innocence and inexperience. It also has connotations of vulnerability. In this way, she is used as a symbol of all of the other vulnerable women who were paid poor wages, and could not work if they spoke out, or became ill or pregnant. This was true in 1912 but also in 1946 in a country filled with war orphans and injured men unable to support their families. Priestley wanted to explore the idea that his own generation had experienced many hardships and so should consider how socialism may help.

6 Write your full essay response in no more than 40 minutes.

Peer- and self-assessment

Assessment objectives
- AO1, AO2, AO3, AO4

1 Read the following essay response to the exam-style question on page 113 and the examiner's annotations.

Student C

Mr Birling is a powerful businessman. His factories and their profit are his priorities throughout the play, not social responsibility. He never feels sorry for sacking Eva and he never accepts the idea that he is connected to her, or to anyone else except his family members. Priestley wanted to show that it is bad to not feel social responsibility. Sometimes this attitude is quite shocking, but it is similar to the attitudes of many employers in 1912, when there were strikes and campaigns for higher pay.

Birling says: 'a man has to mind his own business and look after himself and his own.' He does not believe in social responsibility and just thinks a man should 'look after himself'. The way he uses the word 'has', as if there is no choice, suggests again that this is a strongly held belief of his. It creates the effect that Birling is confident and sure and takes seriously what he considers his responsibilities. Birling rejects the Inspector's socialist ideas, which Priestley supported and wanted the audience to sympathise with.

When asked why he sacked Eva, Mr Birling speaks with confidence and has no doubt that he did the right thing in being focused on profits: 'They were averaging about twenty-two and six, which was neither more nor less than is paid generally in our industry ... we'd have added about twelve per cent to our labour costs.' His use of numbers and amounts makes it clear that it is all about money with Mr Birling, which is what Priestley wants us to realise. Birling does not care about the people and social responsibility, just profit.

AO1 – clear response to task and text

AO3 – clear link and understanding of contextual factors

AO1 – explained response to task with supporting reference

AO2 – clear explanation of the effect of writer's methods

AO3 – clear link and understanding of contextual factors

AO1 – clear response to task and text with supporting references

AO2 – clear explanation of the effect of writer's methods

AO1 – clear understanding of task and text

AO2 – relevant comments on writer's methods with relevant subject terminology

Mr Birling does not get upset about what happened to Eva at all, and says he can't accept 'responsibility'. He only wants to help at the end when he thinks that everyone will find out what his family has done. He offers 'thousands' to the Inspector. This noun implies he has lots of money he could spend. It tells the audience that he could have helped the workers as he had the money but he did not feel social responsibility so he did not.

Overall, social responsibility is shown through Mr Birling because he does not have any. The way he refuses to react to anything except business and money makes him seem unkind and unnatural as if he has taken his responsibility to look after his business too far and forgotten to take responsibility for people. I think this is Priestley's message to the audience, that there is more to being a businessman than just making money.

AO1 – explained response with integrated textual reference

AO1 – explained response

AO1 – clear response to task and text

AO1 and AO3 – clear understanding of ideas and perspectives

Examiner's comment

This is a well-explained AO1 response with many clear points. AO1 quotations and textual references are almost always well chosen and relevant. There is a clear implicit understanding of AO3 context. There is some inappropriate use of informal language and too little AO2 analysis of writer's methods.

2 Evaluate the answer against the level 4 and level 6 marking criteria on pages 126–7 and decide which level you think the response is closer to.

3 Next, read Student D's response and the examiner's annotations.

Student D

J. B. Priestley presents Arthur Birling as a 'responsible businessman' in that he is clearly dedicated to making as much money as possible in order to fulfil his sense of responsibility towards himself and his family. However, we see that he has no desire to look after – or see himself as connected to the welfare of – his employees or anyone else he comes across, so although he is 'responsible' for business, he is not a socially responsible character. Priestley uses Mr Birling to explore what real social responsibility could be for an employer.

AO1 – conceptualised, critical response with integrated supporting references

Even in his engagement speech, Mr Birling hopes for 'lower costs and higher prices' when the Crofts' and Birlings' businesses might work together. His dedication to his business seems inappropriate at such a time, and hints at the way that feelings may not be as important to Mr Birling as money. This is important because it is, of course, human feeling that motivates social responsibility. The audience are being encouraged to feel negatively towards Mr Birling already, as Priestley wants them to question Birling's capitalist values. His lack of sentiment towards his daughter's wedding helps to achieve this.

AO1 – developed, exploratory response with integrated supporting references

AO2 and AO3 – relevant comment on writer's methods with clear link to context

Soon after, Mr Birling mentions the 'wild talk' of labour trouble and dismisses it, claiming that 'the interests of capital' are more important. He's undermined by the dramatic irony, as a 1946 audience knew that there was considerable labour unrest in 1912 and thereafter, and that workers' rights were significantly improved as a result. The adjective 'wild' indicates that he considers the talk to be irrational and even dangerous, helping to depict Birling as someone who sees social responsibility and workers' rights as things that do not matter, highlighting his view that anyone seriously considering such matters is 'wild'.

AO2 and AO3 – explained comment on writer's methods with thoughtful link to context and perspectives

AO2 – examination of writer's methods with accurate subject terminology

When Mr Birling recounts his involvement with Eva Smith, we see the true limits of his 'responsibility'. He says: 'it's my duty to keep labour costs down'. Interestingly, he uses the noun 'duty', implying a strong sense of moral responsibility, while his tone is very dismissive about the workers, later calling them 'these people' as if they are not even worthy of a name. This juxtaposition emphasises how Birling values money over people and believes that his only responsibility lies with profit, regardless of the human cost. Eric's (and later Sheila's) reactions to his attitude suggest that his views were not popular with the younger generation in Edwardian times. Priestley may have been reminding his contemporaries that they should embrace socialism, as they were Sheila and Eric's age at the time the play was set.

AO1 and AO2 – analysis of writer's methods with judicious textual references

AO3 – thoughtful consideration of perspectives linked with context

Examiner's comment

This response is convincingly argued and demonstrates a detailed understanding of the text as well as a critical overview. AO1 points are judiciously supported with apt textual detail and references to AO3 context support and develop ideas and interpretation. The effect of AO2 writer's methods are analysed well.

4 Evaluate this answer and decide which of the two levels (4 or 6) it is closer to. In what ways is this response more effective than Student C's?

Apply what you have learned

Look again at your own work and follow this process:
- ✔ Annotate your work using the Assessment objectives (AOs) as the examiner did for Students C and D.
- ✔ Evaluate the level you think it is closest to.
- ✔ Next, find a paragraph in your work that you think requires improvement or development.
- ✔ Identify which aspects from the AOs you need to improve in your chosen paragraph.
- ✔ Re-draft or rewrite the paragraph, applying the changes you think are needed.

Revision and practice

Checklist for success

Before the exam:
- ✔ Reread the play alongside this book.
- ✔ Watch the play, either in live performance or film.
- ✔ Using this book, select and learn at least three quotations for each character and theme.
- ✔ Make yourself note cards on the characters and key themes, and use them for revision.
- ✔ Practise writing quick plans to practice exam questions.
- ✔ Practise writing essay responses to practice exam questions.

In the exam:
- ✔ Read the question and highlight the key things you are being asked to write about.
- ✔ Write a quick plan, outlining what points you will cover.

Remember:
- ✔ Outline a premise and argue this premise to develop your essay. (AO1)
- ✔ Write in paragraphs, clearly explaining your ideas and giving evidence to support them. (AO1)
- ✔ Use quotations with quotations marks. Keep them short and embed them in your writing if you can. (AO1)
- ✔ Use subject terminology to identify Priestley's methods.
- ✔ Keep your focus on what Priestley does – his use of language and structure and the effect of his choices in relation to the task. (AO2)
- ✔ Consider how Priestley's methods or the events in the play can be interpreted through contextual factors.

Acknowledgements

The publishers gratefully acknowledge the permissions granted to reproduce copyright material in this book. Every effort has been made to contact the holders of copyright material, but if any have been inadvertently overlooked, the Publisher will be pleased to make the necessary arrangements at the first opportunity.

United Agents for extracts from *English Journey,* 1934; *Time and the Conways*, 1937; *Postscripts, BBC radio show*, 1940; *Out of the People*, 1941; *Delight,* 1949; and *Margin Released,* 1962 by J. B. Priestley. Reproduced with permission United Agents on behalf of the Estate of J. B. Priestley; Approximately two thousand words (2000) from *An Inspector Calls* by J. B. Priestley, Penguin Books, 2001, copyright © J. B. Priestley, 1947. Reproduced by permission of Penguin Books Ltd; Mirrorpix for an extract adapted from "Everywoman in 1910: No vote, poor pay, little help – Why the world had to change", *The Mirror*, 08/03/2010, updated 08/03/2013, copyright © Mirrorpix 2010. Reproduced with permission; The British Library for extracts from 'An Appeal Against Female Suffrage' by Mrs Humphrey Ward, published in *The Nineteenth Century Magazine* in June 1889; and *Custodia Honesta* by George Sigerson, pp.5-6, published by The Women's Press 1913, copyright © the British Library. Reproduced by permission of the British Library; Little, Brown Book Group for an extract from *Every Man for Himself* by Beryl Bainbridge, Abacus, 1996, p.211. Reproduced with permission of Little, Brown Book Group; War on Want for an extract from "Sweatshops in Bangladesh", http://www.waronwant.org/sweatshops-bangladesh, copyright © War on Want. Reproduced with permission; and Random House Group Ltd and A M Heath for an extract from *The Complete Works of George Orwell: Volume 1: Down and Out in Paris and London* by George Orwell published by Martin Secker & Warburg Ltd, pp.141-142, copyright © George Orwell, 1933. Reproduced with permission of The Random House Group Ltd © 1986 and A M Heath.

The publishers would like to thank the following for permission to reproduce pictures in these pages:

Cover images: (l) mauritius images GmbH/Alamy Stock Photo, (r) itanistock/Stockimo/Alamy Stock Photo

p9 Bettmann/Getty Images, p10 John Frost Newspapers/Alamy Stock Photo, p12 Chronicle/Alamy Stock Photo, p15a MARKA/ Alamy Stock Photo, p15b IWM/Getty Images, p15c Bletchley Park Trust/Getty Images, p15d Hulton Archive/Getty Images, p16 Pictorial Press Ltd/Alamy Stock Photo, p18l Bettmann/Getty Images, p18r The National Trust Photolibrary/Alamy Stock Photo, p19 Bettmann/Getty Images, p21 Chronicle/Alamy Stock Photo, p22a Everett Collection Inc/Alamy Stock Photo, p22b Heritage Image Partnership Ltd/Alamy Stock Photo, p24a Granger Historical Picture Archive/Alamy Stock Photo, p24b World History Archive/ Alamy Stock Photo, p26 Elizabeth Whiting & Associates/Alamy Stock Photo, p29 INTERFOTO/Alamy Stock Photo, p31 Chronicle/ Alamy Stock Photo, p32 Donald Cooper/Photostage, p33 Donald Cooper/Photostage, p33 Mary Evans Picture Library, p36 The John Williamson Company Ltd., 1898, OOC, p38 Donald Cooper/ Photostage, p40 Donald Cooper/Photostage, p44 Everett Historical/ Shutterstock, p47 Donald Cooper/Photostage, p48 Donald Cooper/ Photostage, p50 Donald Cooper/Photostage, p52 Chronicle/ Alamy Stock Photo, p55 Joerg Boethling/Alamy Stock Photo, p56 Donald Cooper/Photostage, p59 Archive Pics/Alamy Stock Photo, p61 Donald Cooper/Photostage, p63 Donald Cooper/ Photostage, p65 Chronicle/Alamy Stock Photo, p67 Archive Pics/Alamy Stock Photo, p68 History collection 2016/Alamy Stock Photo, p71 Archive Pics/Alamy Stock Photo, p73 Donald Cooper/Photostage, p75 Donald Cooper/Photostage, p79 Jane Hobson/REX/Shutterstock, p82 f8 archive/Alamy Stock Photo, p85 Donald Cooper/Photostage, p86 Donald Cooper/Photostage, p88 Donald Cooper/Photostage, p91 Donald Cooper/Photostage, p92 oliveromg/Shutterstock, p95 Donald Cooper/Photostage, p97 Donald Cooper/Photostage, p99 Donald Cooper/Photostage, p102 Donald Cooper/Photostage, p105 HistoryQuest/Alamy Stock Photo, p109 Donald Cooper/Photostage, p110 Donald Cooper/ Photostage, p111 Donald Cooper/Photostage, p115 Donald Cooper/ Photostage, p117 Donald Cooper/Photostage, p118 vectorfusionart/ Shutterstock, p120 Donald Cooper/Photostage, p121 Gábor Páll/ Alamy Stock Photo.